Stuart MACONIE

NEVER MIND *the* QUANTOCKS

stuart
MACONIE
NEVER MIND *the* QUANTOCKS

How country walking can change your life

David and Charles

CONTENTS

FOREWORD

I started walking in the late 1980s. Well, no, I actually started walking in the mid 1960s, much to the delight I imagine of my mum and dad, and had become really quite adept at it by the late 1980s. What I mean is that I started 'walking' in the late 1980s in the sense that I imagine everyone reading this little tome knows and loves it. By which I mean walking as an end in itself, a lovely, noble, almost artistic endeavour full of pleasure and danger and wonder, as opposed to the quotidian, one foot in front of the other, getting from A to B, pedestrian in every sense, kind of walking.

And when I began that kind of walking, most of my work mates thought I was a nutter. There are two reasons for this. One was the kind of work I did, namely a young-ish writer for hipster rock bible the *NME*. And the other was the general image that 'rambling' (not a sexy or indeed accurate description) was held in up until quite recently. Maybe it was just the culture I grew up in, an urban adolescence of punk rock, girls, Northern soul and generally getting into trouble, but I had reached the ill-informed and lazy conclusion that 'walkers' were dull, middle class bores with facial hair and bad dress sense. I knew nothing then of Benny Rothman and the Kinder Trespass, of Ewan MacColl and the Manchester Rambler, of the Ramblers Society's roots in the love of the working classes for their landscape and their refusal to accept that it belonged to someone else.

No, back then I just thought ramblers were weirdos in bobble hats. If I was dragged on a walk by a well-intentioned mate or girlfriend, I would take a perverse and callow pride in not having the right gear, of going clad in a leather jacket or an overcoat, plastic sandals or espadrilles. I would refuse to look at the map and affect to be unmoved by the view, claiming to be only interested in getting back to the streetlamps of the town and the clamour of the pub and nightclub. In retrospect, I can see that I was bit of a pillock.

Anyway, that all changed one half term in the 1980s when I spent a long weekend in the Lake District. Perhaps because my working life had become a smoky, shouty round of gigs, airports, and overgrown adolescents in black jeans who thought Dungeon Ghyll was a heavy metal band from Wolverhampton. I walked to Easedale Tarn, did the circuit of

Devoke Water and stood at the foot of the path up Brown Tongue to Helvellyn and knew that I had found a romance that would last me the rest of my life

I am probably still a bit of a pillock from time to time. But at least now I'm one who loves to walk. I still love all the delicious, noisy, naughty urban things my teenage self did. And I enjoy them even more after a day on the hills or in the woods or by the river or the sea. Walking for me is a celebration of the joy of being alive, alone or with friends, epic expeditions or easy rambles, as long as it is outside where the free things are (in every sense) and where the perspective on life is longer and clearer and higher. For, as the poet Thom Gunn said 'one is always nearer by not standing still'

Stuart Maconie

INTRODUCTION

I was listening to Stuart's radio show last night, and he apologised for sounding flustered, adding: "I've had to come into the London studio; couldn't get back to Manchester because there was a dead ocelot on the track at Didcot Parkway."

I think that sentence tells you some very important things about Stuart Maconie.

1) His command of language, and habit of making you laugh with it, is absolutely awesome.
2) He loves the north of England and, while he's very happy to explore the South West Coast Path or indeed the Quantocks, it's never long before he wants to get back to, talk about, or explore his beloved home turf.
3) He knows the most amusingly-named station to throw in to an anecdote about rail travel.

These important things have all helped to make his monthly column for *Country Walking* an absolute pleasure to read for the past seven years.

The magazine is devoted to those lucky people who know that Britain is best explored on foot, and Stuart knows that very well. Each month his column looks at some wonderful facet of walking, be it the triumphs and traumas of climbing the Lake District fells beloved of Alfred Wainwright, the joy of exploring the Pennines with a canine companion, conquering the Jurassic Coast with colleague Mark Radcliffe, or heading for the Peak District to walk off a hangover sustained by a night out with the Arctic Monkeys.

He gets the same pleasure out of a canalside stroll as he does from a high-mountain trek. He gets equal pleasure from chatting with a walking companion or being alone amongst the fells with just a teacake for company. And he understands the millions of strangely wonderful moments that walkers encounter every time they set out to put one foot in front of another. Because they've happened to him, too.

In picking up this book, you are taking a stroll with one of Britain's wittiest writers, a peerless storyteller and a genuinely genial guide. Barring any dead ocelots on the path, you'll have a wonderful time with him.

Nick Hallissey
Editor, *Country Walking*

Advice for
Beginners

A nd so, I have decided to give some personal advice to those lucky beginners reading this who stand poised on the great adventure of country walking. Heed my words, walkers of tomorrow!

Gearwise, don't feel you have to straightway buy everything that's reviewed and advertised in the pages of magazines and books. It's all superior stuff I'm sure, but take it in stages, put bits on your birthday list. There is nothing more tragic than seeing the novice walker kitted out from head to toe in the latest breathable technology, clutching an ice axe and clattering polyurethane alpine climbing boots, attempting nothing more taxing than a circuit of the tea shops of Moreton-in-Marsh.

On the other hand, beware false economy. On one of my first walking expeditions, the popular ascent to Easedale Tarn via Sour Milk Ghyll in Grasmere, I decided to augment my meagre kit with a waterproof purchased in the village post office for the frankly irresistible price of £8.

It was a sort of souwester made of dauntingly heavy-duty rubber and was certainly waterproof. I think it would have proved fireproof and radiation-proof, too. By the time I got to the tarn I was drenched in sweat, several pounds lighter, and so hot and dehydrated that in my delirium I fancied I could see a caravan of Tuareg nomads over Greenup Edge.

Tick off a list. Purists and snobs may scoff, but ignore them. Almost as soon as I got the fellwalking bug, I resolved to complete the Wainwrights. A goal like this gives you a galvanising sense of purpose, helps you plan and encourages you to discover and explore new places, rather than stick only to what you know. It doesn't have to be fells. It could be rivers, canals, cathedrals, even the tea shops of Moreton-in-Marsh, but believe me, a list really is a great motivator.

Encourage friends, but don't press-gang them. Remember how it was when your chum or loved one got into golf/vintage traction engines/the operas of Wagner. One man's meat is another man's poison, and one man's exhilarating day on the high hills is another man's unnecessary brush with pneumonia and edition of *Deal or No Deal* missed. Of course, if they really prefer Noel Edmonds to Nethermost Pike, you might want to think about getting new friends.

Learn how to use a map. Being able to visualise in detail how a walk will look and feel, just from glancing at it over a whisky the night before, is both enjoyable and can really impress people. More importantly, learn how to fold a map; those double-siders can be a job for a black belt in origami and you will learn to your cost, grasshopper, that the bit you want is always on the other side.

Never be afraid to turn back. I have turned turning back into an art form. I've actually turned back while still putting my boots on. As the guidebooks say, the hills will be there tomorrow. But as I say, the steak pudding at the Queens Head in Tirril may not be. But by the same token, don't let your lack of experience make you at all timid.

The great outdoors has traps galore for fools, but I think it welcomes the genuinely adventurous. In my early walking days, I would let the odd bit of murk or flake of snow change my plans. Now, though I'm by no means reckless, I tend to press on for a while, or shelter and have a butty and keep a keen eye on the skies. You'll develop a sixth sense for knowing just when it's all getting too much. If you're clinging by your fingernails to the Wastwater Screes in a lightning storm, then it has.

In the end, take advice. But, in the vernacular of the training shoe ad man, just do it. You'll get lost, you'll get soaked, you might even get scared. And you'll love it. See you out there somewhere I hope.

A Matter of
Opinion

Dispiritingly, Cumbria is younger than me. It's 32 years old. A mere whippersnapper. Back in 1974, doubtless over beer and sandwiches and through a thick plume of Player's No 6 smoke, men in suits in a local government office decided to merge Cumberland and Westmorland, pinch a bit of Furness and the West Riding and, like magicians, conjure up England's loveliest county.

Now I can already hear the cries of dissent emanating from Devon, from Cornwall, from Derbyshire and Suffolk and Northumberland. Yes, these are beautiful places all. In the end it's a matter of opinion, and nothing divides like beauty. For me, what gives Cumbria the edge is the contrasts. Most walkers will know the grandeur and drama of the Lakeland peaks, the shattered ridges and high tarns. But if you want pastoral charm, dinky cottages and soft, rolling lowlands, you will find them in Cumbria's Lyth Valley, where the damsons grow plump and purple.

Fans of Kate Bush and Emily Brontë can find plenty to brood about on the lonely rain-lashed moors of Alston, Cross Fell and the Howgills, whilst connoisseurs of the seascape can feel spray on their face and look over glittering Morecambe Bay to the Isle of Man, or hear the wheeling gulls at lonely Skinburness. If you want to see the side that no-one ever does, take the coastal train. You will wonder, as it clanks through winnowy dunes between the stolid bulk of the south-western fells and the barren coastline, just how Dr Beeching's axe could have missed this line. A clerical error maybe, but a happy one.

Of course, there are parts of Cumbria that these days make Blackpool look reserved and serene. I'm no enthusiast for red tape and excessive regulations – and neither am I one of those nimby's that wants all the nice parts of the country to themselves – but someone really needs to do something about Keswick. While one by one the butchers and fishmongers have shut up shop, discount gear shops have grown like a rash across the town. In mid-summer, the clack of walking poles on pavement is deafening and the rustle of Gore-Tex can be heard in every pie shop.

But this is carping. Great chunks of the county are, but for the odd pub and farm, blissfully empty. Considering its size and the fact that it has tourist attractions galore, from Peter Rabbit to Sellafield, it may be England's least known county, certainly outside of the outdoor fraternity. Go to the fringes and you can walk for days without seeing another soul. Even inside the Lake District National Park boundary, if you choose your day and route with care, you hardly have to doff a cap or exchange a pleasantry all day.

No need to be like that, though. You'll find the natives are very friendly. The accent – a sort of Lancashire-Geordie-Lowland Scots – can take some getting used to and the dialect is peppered with Norse, like 'clarty' and 'lal' and 'ladgeful' for dirty, little and embarrassing respectively. But Cumbrian people are generally tough, resourceful and good-humoured. And surprising; the farmer near me in Hutton Roof will pass by with merely a nod of the head for months and then, apropos of nothing more than a squall of rain, keep you for an hour by his gatepost.

Not convinced? Then this is how the entry for Cumbria ends in a well-known online encyclopaedia: 'Cumbria is a fun place to visit, especially if you run into Ellie Cook. She is quite possibly the nicest girl in the world and will make a man very happy one day!' Her county will do for me.

The Walking Bug

As soon as anyone starts talking about 'being bitten by the walking bug', some of us will start to scratch our ankles, whinge and hunt out the calomine lotion. Just as some of us are lucky enough to be irresistible to the opposite sex, so some of us are unfortunate enough to prove alluring beyond reason to midges, mosquitoes, tics, fleas, wasps, mites, gnats, giraffe weevils and horned hickory devils.

That's a subject for another day, though. Here I'm talking about a much more pleasant bug and a much more agreeable bite; that moment when you first realise that rambling, scrambling and generally wandering about in the great outdoors is something you'll be doing for the rest of your life.

Saul saw the light on the road to Damascus. Not a particularly exciting road compared to Walna Scar or the A817 from Loch Lomond to Garelochhead, but it was enough to convert him. It's a matter of walker's lore that Alfred Wainwright's Damascene conversion, from faintly grumpy Blackburn Rovers terrace dweller to patron saint of the high places, came on a visit to a little hill above the village of Windermere.

Aged 23 in 1930, he climbed Orrest Head and later wrote that, 'those few hours cast a spell that changed my life.' He was to move to Kendal, write the bibles of fellwalking, and become the most famous anorak wearer in the world after Oasis' Liam Gallagher.

For Wainwright it was Orrest Head. With me it was the Queen's Head in Hawkshead. Actually, that's far too glib, though it was teenage fishing trips to the Lakes accompanied by copious amounts of illicit drinking. I didn't really have my Orrest Head moment for a few more years.

It came, like a lot of people's does, on Loughrigg Fell, after the short, stiff pull up from Loughrigg Terrace. Gulping lungfuls of air on a balmy summer's afternoon, I saw the fells of the central Lakes arrayed in the hazy blue distance. It was truly magical, an elevated experience in the literal and spiritual sense, and I knew as I stood there with a faraway smile on my face, that this was something I'd do again and again as long as my legs and lungs would allow.

It was love at first sight. The eyes-across-a-crowded-room moment beloved of romantic novelists. Not reciprocated of course. I have no idea what Crinkle Crags thought of me, but I was smitten. What was the initial attraction? A sense of otherness I suppose, a sense of being suddenly beyond the dull constraints of ordinary life, the traffic jams, the train delays, the stuffy offices and the factory gates.

With their unbeatable 'Ta-da!' factor, mountains are the perfect place to get the walking bug. They're real head-turners. But you can get the bug anywhere.

WH Auden went on a childhood holiday to the Northern Pennines, now an Area of Outstanding Natural Beauty, but then an overlooked bit of semi-industrial limestone country, and found his spiritual home. He dropped a stone down a disused mineshaft, waited for the splash, and in that moment of silent boyhood wonder, began the ripples that run right through his poetry.

You can tell when someone has got the bug. And when someone remains unbitten and immune. Time after time, I've taken a friend walking and, on our return, they've said 'that was nice' or words to that effect, but you know by the look in their eyes that they are not infected. By contrast, you know immediately, by the way they demand to borrow your guidebooks, or ask you to identify distant hills, that they are in the thrall of the love affair, too.

Every one of us knows the moment when the simple act of putting one foot in front of another stops being a method of propulsion and becomes an adventure. And wherever we are, just like Arnie, we know we'll be back.

Right to Roam

A while ago, as we headed south down the M6 and crested the summit of Shap Fell at 69mph (officer), we noticed with some pleasure and surprise that we had several hours of weekend left and that it had turned into a really rather fine Sunday evening in Cumbria. So we pulled in by the Shap memorial, dedicated to the haulage heroes of the old arterial road who braved snow and fog and ice to take sausages and hats and washing powder to Dumfries, pulled on the boots and went for an impromptu walk.

The fences and barbed wire and lack of footpaths would have put me off once, but not now. For on my new Explorer series map, all of these lonely moorland heights from Little Yarlside to Whatshaw Common are now coloured a sickly yellow. The hue is unappealing but the message gladdens the heart. Thanks to recent legislation, these are now access areas and, though the gates may be padlocked, you and I have the right to roam. So roam we did, 'til the hum of the traffic receded and the cold got into our bones and the sun dropped behind the Howgills.

That sickly yellow has become my favourite colour. I love the warm glow of satisfaction that it brings. I don't think of myself as some Che Guevara of the hills. I don't think all property is theft – I quite like my iPod, for instance. But there is something about the notion of 'trespass', particularly on the high hills, that has always irritated me. What possible harm could I be doing, I've always thought? My anorak is made by Dolce and Gabbana and I always take my pork pie wrapper home with me.

Of course, my mere presence might be an affront to some. They say an Englishman's home is his castle so maybe an Englishman's back garden is his empire, even when that Englishman is an ageing rebel. Rolling Stone Keith Richards initially wanted to keep ramblers away from a field adjoining his Redlands mansion in Sussex, scene of one of the infamous 'sleepovers' of the 1960s.

Now, of all people, Keith should know that a walk a day helps you work, rest and play. Happily, he withdrew his application. Madonna is neither a man nor English, but she wanted to stop the Open Access legislation applying to a small patch of her Wiltshire estate. Having seen her last movie with Guy Ritchie I'd have thought she'd want any audience she could get. But what do I know?

Then of course, there's Nicholas Van Hoogstraten, multi-millionaire property developer, robust landlord and friend of Robert Mugabe. One of Hoogstraten's lesser misdeeds was to unlawfully obstruct a footpath on his vast estate near Uckfield. This was to keep us ramblers at bay since he thinks we're all 'perverts'.

Mind you, he also once declared, 'I don't believe in democracy. I believe in rule by the fittest,' and that, 'The only purpose in creating great wealth like mine is to separate oneself from the riff-raff.' That's us, kids. Riff-raff with rucksacks, the worst kind.

The grumpy old man in me fears that the 'younger generation' probably think that the Kinder Trespass is some kind of offshoot of the Kinder Egg, an odd German kind of chocolate trespass containing a cheap plastic gift.

But to many, it's the defining moment, the red letter day, the crowning glory of the walking fraternity that in 1932 united the ramblers' cause to obtain greater access to roam across the country.

After all, a very senior authority, more senior some would contend than any landowner, lawyer or rambler, did once say, 'Forgive us our trespasses, as we forgive those who trespass against us.' Madonna and Keith and Old Nick – he will surely join his more senior namesake one day – should maybe remember that.

Carry On Camping!

Camping. What a carry on! But a carry on that doesn't even offer the meagre entertainment value of Sid James chortling whilst Babs Windsor loses her bra doing some PT exercises. Tin mugs, rehydrated pasta, queuing for shower blocks. Can't you just feel that involuntary shudder?

Call me a snob, but anywhere that doesn't have a microwave and a device for crushing ice counts as camping in my book. And my book, by the way, would be *The Great Gatsby* rather than the *Which? Guide to Camping and Caravanning*. That was what I used to think, anyway.

These thoughts came back to me the night that found me pacing around a flattish square of rough ground by the shores of Sprinkling Tarn, in the Lake District, wondering where to pitch my tent and actually using, out loud, phrases like 'adequate drainage' and 'degree of slope'.

Later, as I ate my aforementioned rehydrated pasta by the glimmer of a smouldering mosquito coil, I wondered at just which point I had gone mad and gone back on the cosy and sophisticated habits of a lifetime.

That night, my first wild camp ever, was, without doubt the most uncomfortable night I have ever spent; and I have been on tour with Birmingham Grunge-Metal outfit Napalm Death by the way.

Yet not only have I repeated it, voluntarily, I shall be doing it all again with a spring in my step as soon as possible. No, I didn't sleep. Yes, it was awkward and smelly.

Yes, I missed my G&T. No, I didn't ever really manage to get the hang of the sleeping bag zip attachment. And yes, I did keep rolling to one side of the tent and find my ear poking out from under the fly-sheet.

But all of these discomforts evaporated when, on finding myself needing what the Americans would call 'a comfort break' at around 6am, I muttered an apology to my smugly sleeping wife, shuffled on my hands and knees toward the tent opening and whipped back the zip.

There before me was the huge and imposing wall of Great End. Barely glimpsed last night through the evening murk, it was now, bizarrely and gorgeously, pink from the first rays of the sun. It looked like God's Christmas cake or a giant Pet Shop Boys stage decoration, both monumentally awesome and a little camp, looking down on our little camp.

It was one of the most glorious sights I have ever seen. Moving like a zombie, it lured me from the fug of the tent, walking damp-footed through the dewy grass. Turning I saw Sprinkling Tarn shining like a newly-minted coin in its rocky bowl and beyond it, Seathwaite was filled with cloud like a pill bottle stuffed with cotton wool.

Suddenly, it all made sense. I knew why people deserted their soft beds and ice-crushers and drinks cabinets. I knew why the people who'd been coming down from the hill the night before had looked at us a little enviously when we said we were 'spending the night up there.'

I knew it even more profoundly when, an hour later, while people were still eating their toast and checking the weather forecast in Keswick, we were on top of Great End, looking down at the drowsy morning world.

I still don't see the appeal of organised site camping, unless you're on a budget. The cars and the cramped sites and the shower blocks still give me that shudder. But I'll go wild camping again as soon as I can. And so should you. It is damp and sticky and uncomfortable. And you will absolutely love it.

Seeds of
Destruction

On an unseasonably hot Sunday in spring, I set out to climb Clough Head in the Lake District, by the forbidding looking but tantalisingly named Fisher's Wife's Rake. Then, according to my announced itinerary, I would spend the best part of the day heading south along the undulating whalebacks of the Dodds before descending Sticks Pass and getting my pre-arranged lift to Keswick where beer and curry awaited.

That was the plan and I was pleased with it. But just as Karl Marx said, wrongly as it turned out, that capitalism carried within it the seeds of its own destruction, so I carried with me my own downfall in the shape of a portable radio, a really nice organic sausage and mash pie and the knowledge that Wigan Athletic were playing Tottenham Hotspur in a vital relegation clash at the JJB stadium that day.

That, and the heat, and the fact that even the short pull up the quarry track had me mopping sweat from my brow, meant that a new and attractive plan soon occurred to me. Namely, walk the Matterdale Coach Road, find a nice spot, eat pie, sunbathe, doze and carry on into Dockray where a cold pint of beer had, I felt sure, my name on it.

Now I don't feel bad about that. Walking is about fun not duty. I was out in my favourite landscape with the sun on my face and the sound of lark song all around, albeit vying for supremacy with Alan Green's commentary on BBC Five Live. I didn't mind this at all. As the blessed

Alfred Wainwright nearly said, the fells are eternal, but Wigan may well not be in the Premiership by the time you read this. AW founded the Blackburn Rovers Supporters Club and would have understood. I didn't feel guilty. I just felt stupid. Which is why I hid myself in a grassy hollow far from the track and every time a fellow walker passed, would cover the radio with an OS Map which I pretended to be studying intently.

It just felt wrong. Faintly city-ish and silly and certainly something a real walker wouldn't do, like doing Striding Edge in slingbacks or an Armani suit. When David Beckham scored his famous redemptive penalty against Argentina in the 2002 World Cup, myself, my wife, two friends and their kids were all glued to the match on a hand-held telly atop Hallin Fell (our cottage had no electricity), but we were all vaguely embarrassed, and pretended to be admiring a mountain flower or rock formation when anyone passed.

It's crazy really. Walking shouldn't have rules. If it will get them out and about in the fresh air, let your kids take their PlayStation or Nintendo DS with them, let Kylie take her iPod and let dad take his radio pressed to his ear. None of these things are any more offensive than the wannabe Jeremy Clarksons in their off-roaders who churn these lovely places in their hateful 4x4s. Or those hearty Baden Powell types who feel it necessary to shout out the names of every peak in stentorian, self-satisfied tones. Compared to these, I was discretion and quietude itself, blending into

the verdant slopes, head on my rucksack, radio by my ear.
Until Tottenham scored their winner of course...

Hanging Around

Crosby is a pleasant suburb at the mouth of the Mersey, the most desirable place to live in the environs of Liverpool it's said, and rich with associations to the Titanic disaster, being home to the doomed skipper Edward Smith and the lucky owner of the White Star line, Bruce Isme, who got a seat in one of the lifeboats.

When I was a kid, Crosby was a good place to come for a Sunday afternoon stroll. We could be here from my gran's in urban Lancashire in under an hour and, butties and flask in hands, could walk along the dunes for hours, gleefully getting sand in our sarnies and looking out across the glittering estuary as the seabirds wheeled noisily overhead.

Come to Crosby now – twilight is best – and you'll see a remarkable thing: 100 life-sized cast-iron figures gazing out to sea, some waist-high in the tide, all of them expectant, silent and melancholy. This is *Another Place*, an installation by sculptor Anthony Gormley and it is inexpressibly moving. Other people seem to agree; like Gormley's most famous work, the *Angel of the North*, the reaction from the public has been overwhelmingly positive. Visitors come in their thousands to see the piece, a fact which I for one find tremendously heartening.

Fustian fuddy-duddies like Brian Sewell and the leader writers of the *Daily Mail* probably hate things like *Another Place*. They think sculpture should be some Greek god with undernourished crown jewels on a plinth in a dusty gallery. They certainly don't think art should be just hanging around where you might discover it on a country walk. In theory it might seem odd, but in practice it can add a new dimension to your experience of landscape and place.

Take Grizedale Forest Sculpture Park in the Lakes. Yes, there's a big wooden Viking in the car park for the kids to 'coo' over, but some of the other treats are more subtle. Pat Leighton's *Vigil*, for example, located deep in the heart of the forest and seemingly part of it at first, a skein of fabric and wood hung high in a tree that, as the artist says, 'feels as if it purposefully belonged to its placing in the landscape, emitting a sense of timelessness... monumentality and mystery.'

This may sound like the sort of thing artists always say, but it perfectly sums up how I felt about *Vigil* when I first saw it on a gloomy November afternoon. Some sculpture park exhibits, though, deliberately play on their shock value and their lack of fit in the landscape. I love the moment at Yorkshire Sculpture Park – probably the finest in Britain and home to a fabulous collection of Barbara Hepworth and Henry Moore works – when the casual stroller spots, written on a high tree branch across the path, the word 'UNNATURAL' in bright neon lettering, a witty piece by Sean Pickard that seems a riposte to all the harrumphers who think proper art is a painting of a bowl of fruit.

If nothing else, environmental art is better for you. I did once jog round the Uffizi gallery having misread the closing times and being desperate to get my fix of old masters, but generally you won't get fit looking for art. Unless it's someone like Andy Goldsworthy, who alongside

Gormley is the finest exponent of this new environmental installation art.

Goldsworthy builds giant cones in forests, makes paths and cairns in far-flung locales, rebuilds remote ruined sheepfolds to beautiful designs and scatters branches, pebbles and seaweed along deserted beaches. Traditionalists may mock, but come across work like this when you're out on an evening stroll, or at daybreak, or in the depths of a winter storm, and you may not know about art, but you know that you like it.

High Expectations

It is better to travel hopefully than to arrive, said Robert Louis Stevenson. This suggests that he was familiar with the UK railway network in the 90s, but that's not actually what he meant. What Bob was trying to convey was that it is the expectation, the sense of anticipation, the process of getting to somewhere that is often the best bit of travel, not the destination. Taoist philosophy has a similar adage: 'The journey is the reward.'

That's interesting to me at this very moment as I'm in a fast car watching the sun set over the Howgill Fells as I race up the M6 to Edinburgh. Don't worry, I'm not driving. I'm tucked up in the back with my laptop and boiled sweets and magazines, being driven to a late rendezvous with a big comfy bed on the Royal Mile and tomorrow an ascent of Arthur's Seat, for a travel show I'm doing for TV.

And I know what Robert L meant. Of course I'd rather be there now, in my fluffy robe, sipping a fine old malt propped up on implausibly fluffy pillows. But there is something about travel itself, the sense of movement, the impermanence, that's thrilling. Generally anyway. But there are exceptions.

A few years back I took the fabled London to Scotland sleeper, a source of romance to generations of readers and movie fans. The journey was taken at the instigation of a TV director I was making a show with in Glasgow and who was frightened of flying. I would have been happy with the plastic glass of in-flight G&T, the little bag of nuts and the hour in the sky but thought to myself, hey, it's an experience.

To be honest my expectations were way too high; I thought that Robert Donat would be on board, or at least Margaret Rutherford. I imagined crisply uniformed staff mixing me a Martini and falling into conversation with a beautiful and mysterious Russian heiress who appeared to be avoiding some burly bearded men who kept disappearing behind their newspapers. I rather hoped to find a dead body in my bunk and to be wrongly arrested on arrival in Glasgow, but that it would all turn out right in the end.

Actually it was a bit like what I imagine prison is like, but on wheels. Convenient enough, but functional rather than nostalgic. No gaslights or starched white waistcoats. Just a little covered sink and a couple of coat hangers. Subsequently the night passed slowly as we chugged through sleeping Crewe and Carlisle. And it was too dark to see anything anyway.

Now if you are heading north and it's during the day and you are pretty blasé about carbon footprints and global warming, then the plane is an attractive option for three reasons these days. One: if you're lucky, you'll get a ticket for 14p, though naturally you won't get the little bag of nuts with Poundland Airlines. Two: it's quick and will extend that valuable weekend.

Best of all, ask for a seat on the left on the way out and the right on the way back like I always do. They'll give you a funny look but you won't mind when you're looking down on the grandeur of the Fairfield Horseshoe or Blencathra, or the tiny figures toiling up Striding Edge from your eyrie in the sky. That is almost better than arriving. You won't even miss the nuts.

The Essentials

I like Ray Mears. He's the kind of guy you'd like to have around when things go pear-shaped. If your tent fell into a crevasse on the North Face of the Eiger, or you broke your ankle coming off Jack's Rake and slid all the way into Stickle Tarn, he's the kind of bloke you'd want alongside you, as opposed to, say, Jeremy Clarkson or Simon Cowell.

Mearsy, as I like to think people call him, is my kind of outdoor survival expert; no beard, no macho guff, thoughtful, unflappable and appreciative and respectful of the landscape around him. If you did end up screaming in pain in Stickle Tarn, I'm sure that he could rustle you up a pretty serviceable splint and stretcher from some bog sedge, reeds and bits of wool plucked from a passing Herdwick. Also, and this I really like him for, I once saw him make an ice cube from frozen birch sap. He said that one was perfect in a glass of very good malt whisky.

Survival in extremis seems to be a matter of knowing some neat tricks and knots and handholds and such, and carrying the 'essentials'.

Nearly every book on fellwalking contains the obligatory chapter on essentials. This is a mantra we know; emergency food, extra layer, whistle, torch, etc. But most of the books say that for winter walks, ice axe and crampons are essential. I have some crampons but I have never worn them. Their sole purpose is to jab me in the small of the back when I put my rucksack on at a certain angle. I don't have an ice axe. Moreover, I'm tempted to think that me taking the ice axe out on a winter walk would increase rather than minimise the risk of danger. I just know that through a series of freak circumstances I would cut a foot off before I'd even got out of the big car park in Keswick.

Ever conscious of the fellwalkers' insatiable appetite for daft bits of kit and their need to spend money when the rain pins them down in Cotswold or Blacks or George Fisher for an afternoon, manufacturers now make things like survival bars. The original survival bar – though never marketed as such – was the Kendal Mint Cake and, if a little hard and sugary, I still prefer it to those things that taste like the solidified material found at the bottom of a budgie cage.

If you're very enterprising, you can make your own survival bar. I have just looked up a recipe on the internet. There are eight different ingredients which have to be mixed, pressed into shape, cooked at a low heat for three-quarters of an hour and then completely dried before being included amongst one's rations. I'm tempted to say that if you're obsessive, it might be better to devote a little of the time spent making and drying survival bars into not having an accident, but I suppose that's unfair.

In my approach to essentials and survival, I fancy I'm more Rufus Wainwright than Alfred. For one summer's wild camp above Eskdale for instance, 'essentials' included a small bottle of Rioja, some scented wipes and a transistor radio so that we could listen to the Proms. I can already hear the mocking laughter of bearded men in Arran sweaters. But to me those items were just as essential as some horrible dried fruit bar or waterproof matches.

Explaining the scented wipes to the mountain rescue team might be a little embarrassing, but at least I'd smell nice as they carried me down.

TV Towns

Holmfirth is a small, pleasant Pennine town of stone cottages nestling between the River Holme and the River Ribble. It's a nice spot, although if you're a keen walker you'll find wilder spots nearby like Holme Moss or even the edges of the Peak District.

For reasons I won't go into here, I once ended up in Holmfirth with Billy Bragg, professional Cliff Richard-alike and Radio One jock Mike Read and one of Jive Bunny. I wasn't alone. Any day of the year, tourists arrive in droves to munch ice creams in the town's bus shelters. And the reason for this popularity is three superannuated geriatric layabouts and their seemingly endless plans to build a flying machine from an old bath.

Last of the Summer Wine is the reason the crowds come to Holmfirth, hoping to catch a sight of Foggy or Shaggy (no, wait, that's Scooby Doo) or whatever they're called. Actually, this part of the world is ripe with these toothsome locations beloved of TV directors.

Down the road is Slaithwaite, (Slawit to the locals), a lovely little town with a canal running down its main street and home to a number of evocatively named pubs such as the Shoulder of Mutton and The Silent Woman. To fans of the gentle drama *Where the Heart Is*, however, it has another name: Skelthwaite.

Head north up the county and you'll find that Goathland is a stolid rather than charming village, though scenically situated and with a stop on the North York Moors Railway. Tourists again flock here because for the past 15 years or sos it has doubled as Aidensfield in the nostalgiafest that is *Heartbeat*.

Us real walkers tend to get sniffy about these places. Canny marketing has turned many of these spots into what I believe are called 'destinations' but the people who head there tend to be the coach parties and the daytrippers; the hordes, as we unkindly like to think of them. Walkers can be a little snobbish about these types of tourist, believing ourselves to be rugged individualists who spurn the crowds and seek solitary bliss. This does seem a little absurd if you've ever seen the queues for Striding Edge on a Bank Holiday Monday.

Also, you might be denying yourself some real treats. Alnwick Castle and the surrounding countryside is beautiful, even if it has become even more crowded than ever since it became Hogwarts in the *Harry Potter* movies. Cheshire's Lyme Park is delightful, I'm told, even if it has become three times more popular since Colin Firth got his shirt damp in the lake there.

The power of TV is nowhere better seen than in the strange case of *Balamory*. The titular village of the kooky children's favourite is in reality Tobermory on the Isle of Mull. It has previous TV form, of course, because of the Womble of the same name, but since *Balamory* started to film there, visitor numbers have increased by 40 per cent and it now contributes £5 million a year to the tourist economy of Mull and the Western Islands. The islanders aren't complaining much.

For me, if TV shows encourage people to explore these lovely islands, or the wild and romantic *Poldark* country in Cornwall, or the honeyed stone elegance of Stamford (aka *Middlemarch*), and forego the greasy burgers in the Chas 'n' Dave bar in Fuengirola – it does exist, believe me – then all the better.

The fact that I filmed a TV show called *Stuart Maconie's TV Towns* doesn't come into it. We may have even increased visitor numbers to the Gateshead car park where Michael Caine killed Alf Roberts in *Get Carter*. But I don't think the likes of Tobermory and Holmfirth need worry just yet.

A Bolshie Goat

Before you think me a total wuss, as I will appear below, first let me make some things perfectly clear. In many matters to do with the animal kingdom, I am more Jamie Oliver than David Attenborough. Take, for instance, the cows that tried to trample me whilst I was fishing on the banks of the River Severn as a teenager. I sincerely hope that they all ended up providing delicious sirloin for the good citizens of Shropshire. Similarly, I trust that the bolshie goat that used to hang around and headbutt you for your crisps outside the Woolpack Inn in Eskdale found its way into a delicious curry for Cumbria's small expatriate Jamaican community. And don't get me started on those bulls in Mitredale.

I'm unabashed about all this. My wife is a vegetarian and I've become as adept at making an asparagus risotto as anyone from Wigan has any right to be, but I believe in the sanctity of the food chain. Things smaller and tastier than me, as long as humanely kept, are mine to eat, just as, in the fullness of time, I shall be eaten by worms as predicted in that fine old philosophical number 'On Ilkley Moor Baht' Hat'.

And yet... most evenings over the summer, you could have found me 'cooing' and 'ahhing' over a new family who'd moved in next door to me in the Lake District. Nice family, noisy at night and prone to midnight feasts, but always nice to see them scurrying back and forth beneath my verandah. Who'd have thought that someone who once got stuck in a lift with Iggy Pop and broke up a fight between Blur and M People could take so much pleasure watching hedgehogs eating overpriced muesli at an hour of night when he could have been drinking Jack Daniels in the Groucho Club?

But no. I think I'm going soft. I've bought a hedgehog house and everything, and we stand by the open window, willing them to go in. We also get unreasonably excited when we see evidence that red squirrels have been to the feeder although we've only seen one once, one misty June dawn. These sightings, though, are to me what white tigers and dolphins and rhinos are to some people: pulse-quickening moments. For me, at the risk of sounding parochial, it's about their quintessential Englishness.

Hedgehogs – short-sighted, diffident, quiet, slightly bumbling and daft – seem to me to embody a pre-Jeremy Kyle Britain before idiocy and shouting and mawkish displays of sentiment were the norm.

A hedgehog, one imagines, is not that bothered about WAGS or TV talent shows or Gordon Ramsay. The red squirrel, on the other hand, is a flash of Arthurian glamour from the old Avalon; shy and beautiful and sadly passing from our world thanks to our stupidity and lack of understanding of nature. When the last red squirrel dies in these islands, as it will within my lifetime I am sure, another bit of colour and joy will have passed from life and future generations will point to Beatrix Potter and the Tufty Club and ask about these creatures, as exotic as unicorns.

They say there's a pine marten in Greystoke Forest and I really hope there is. I'll never see it, which is just as well considering how badly my species have treated it, but I like to think that it's there, slinking through the quiet nights along the trails back to its tree root den. One of the hundreds of pairs of eyes and twitching noses that spot me going by, clumsy and noisy, before going back to their more important business.

Isotonic or Gin and Tonic?

Here then is your starter for ten; what comes in varieties called isotonic, hypertonic and hypotonic? No, not those columns in ancient Greece. No, nothing to do with gymnastics, triangles or atmospheric pressure. They are, as smug and well-hydrated listeners will doubtless know, different types of sports drink.

I did know the difference for about ten minutes. But it's gone. Something to do with sweating from what I remember, so perhaps it's as well we don't dwell on it. Don't sweat, they glow of course. And each of the aforementioned drinks are essentially water with a dash of lemon juice and a pinch of salt.

We might like to think that we walkers are not as susceptible to jargon and marketing as Lycra-clad joggers, mountain bikers and the like. We know H20 when we see it and sup it. But that said, I remember being taken aback when I realised that the 'rehydration systems' on sale in the walking shops were, basically, plastic bags with a length of tube attached.

That didn't stop me from using one for a while, though, until I realised that mine was never going to lose its unappealing plasticky taste and that a bottle filled with tap water was pretty much unimprovable as an effective 'rehydration system'.

In the comfort of home – mine or anyone else's – I'm pretty daring and sophisticated where tinctures are concerned. I can do a mean Moscow Mule or a gorgeous peach smoothie. But I'm a puritanical soul as far as drinks on the hill go. I even find tap water rather cosmopolitan, preferring to drink from becks and streams.

Before the letters start arriving, I should say that I do know all about cryptosporidium – actually that's a lie, I know it's a nasty little devil and that's about it – but there's something about the crystalline gush of a waterfall on a hot day that compels me to stick my head under it.

Other than that my on-the-move libation of choice is coffee. Tea doesn't work in a flask if you ask me. And my coffee is legendary. The secret is to make it strong and sweet. Even people who don't take sugar find it somehow reassuring in a thin drizzle. Also, make sure your Thermos has two large dents in it; it just tastes better that way.

But now we come to the really thorny issue: alcohol. Nine times out of ten, I'd prefer gin and tonic to Isotonic, but that tenth time is when I'm out on the hill. I'm not prissy about these things but generally it just seems wrong, like having a crafty fag in church. But I am willing to make an exception for the traditional, ritual dram taken from the hip flask on arrival at the snowy summit in winter. Bliss.

And before I get too sanctimonious, let me tell you about the glorious spring day when El, Colin and I climbed Dow Crag. Colin is legendary in our circle for his somewhat austere and obtuse approach to preparation. On this particular ascent, he was carrying not a rucksack but a piece of kit that was, in essence, a sheet of tarpaulin tightened at the neck with a rope. It resembled something a badly equipped Romanian army unit might have used in the early 1950s.

On arriving at the summit, the day had grown mild and clear and we had grown hot and thirsty. Out came our banana sandwiches and water. Out of Colin's pack came an entire packet of Ryvita and two cans of Stones bitter. He looked a little shamefaced at this frugal, distinctly 'chavvy' repast and eventually, and rather sheepishly, offered me the can. To humour him, I took a drink.

It was heavenly. nectar and ambrosia and all those other lovely things rolled into one. I wouldn't dream of doing it again. Suppose someone saw me? But however dreadful it looked, I can tell you now that, as an accompaniment to a view over sparkling tarns to a blue ridge of hills, a can of supermarket beer chilled for an hour or three at 2,000 feet, is the *vorsprung durch technic* of rehydration technology.

SAD

'Some symptoms are similar to classic depression: the feeling of sadness, feelings of hopelessness, helplessness, even worthlessness and not deriving the usual pleasure from enjoyable things such as hobbies. The uncommon symptoms… often result in an increase in appetite and excessive sleeping. Fortunately for people afflicted it is treatable. The three major methods of treatment are light therapy, psychotherapy and anti-depressants.'

If any of the above sounds familiar, then maybe you're feeling more SAD than just sad. Seasonal Affective Disorder, unshakeable feelings of gloom and depression at the onset of winter, is now recognised as a very real psychological condition and not just 'the winter blues'. Sufferers can get some relief from medication and by sitting in front of lightboxes and soaking up the serotonin-inducing rays, but for those afflicted, the clocks going back and the coming of short winter days is always a melancholy time. Philip Larkin, laureate of gloom, had it just right at the end of his marvelously lugubrious poem *Toads Revisited*: 'When the lights come on at four/At the end of another year?/Give me your hand, old toad;/Help me down Cemetry Road.'

But why not look on the bright side. Literally. Let us sing the praises of the short, vibrant days. For one thing, much of our native wildlife loves them. In their wonderful little book of 1974, *Lakeland Mammals* – out of print but of course available on the internet – Mitchell and Delap write movingly about how deer, squirrels and the like are pinned, hungry and nervous, under cover during the 'massive days' of June and July when clumsy humans go crashing through the woods and fields till the late evening. At least when the short days come, such timid creatures can snuffle and forage with confidence in the damp, shadowy undergrowth of a chilly evening knowing that even the keenest walkers will by now be safely indoors watching Julia Bradbury looking winsome on Haystacks.

Short days focus the mind. If you're going to do anything substantial you have to be up early, which is how even a confirmed stay-in-bed like me came to be halfway up Blencathra at 8.30am with the stars still glittering over Sharp Edge not long since. And, as if mindful of their brief bloom, the days themselves go out in an amber blaze of glory, turning even the humble country park into a glowing, radiant epiphany.

Walking at 3.30pm one New Year's Eve on Ling Fell, that homely, shy Christmas Pudding of a hill overlooking Wythop Moss in Northern Cumbria, I was struck quite suddenly by the elegiac loveliness of the twilight, full of the coming dark but revelling in what Tennyson in the *Idylls of the King* called 'The long glories of the winter moon.' Nice phrase. They knew what they were doing, did Tennyson and Larkin. And then what could be nicer than a dram by a fire in a pub somewhere knowing that the evening stretches before you?

I just googled for 'short day winter walks' and the very first I found listed Ben Vrackie near Pitlochry, 'a fine Scottish Corbett only half an hour north of Perth and, with a classic inn for a fine late lunch by a roaring fire at the start/finish point, a great short hill for this time of year.' Now guess what? I've been asked to take part in a Winter Words festival in Pitlochry. My feet are beginning to itch and my acceptance is in the e-mail outbox. As Kylie, Napoleon and that other fine Scottish Corbett Ronnie would attest, short can be beautiful.

Get Jiggy With It

'There are many kinds of love,' remarks Diane Keaton as the Countess in Woody Allen's *Love and Death*. 'There's love between a man and a woman; between a mother and son…' Woody then goes on to include his favourite, which is perhaps a little cheeky for some readers so you'll have to watch the movie.

What he didn't say was the love between two ramblers. We suffer from a bad press in this regard. I think it may be the clothes. Breathable layers and Gore-Tex don't lend themselves to sudden bouts of passion (though, as some of you may even now be acknowledging with a blush, it can be done). That said, I can't be the only person to have watched a certain of the alfresco love scenes in the 90s TV adaptation of Melvyn Bragg's *A Time to Dance*, namely the one on the summit of Grasmoor in deepest winter, and thought, 'I like this novel, Melv, and I admire your optimism, but I've seen more believable episodes of *Battlestar Galactica*.'

Let's turn our mind away from matters carnal though. It's the romance of the outdoors and thoughts of love that occupies us here. And this is the stuff of real romance, too, whatever Richard Curtis may think. Hugh Grant muttering and stammering to Andi MacDowell about *The Partridge Family* pales into trite insignificance against blood red skies over the Cuillin, or morning mist rising from Buttermere seen from Fleetwith Pike, or the rolling patchwork of fields stretching from Bredon to the Malverns and on to Wales. There is something in these sights that makes the heart swell, especially if seen with a kindred soul.

It's no wonder that the original Romantic movement, the first time the word came to general usage in Britain, was about Wordsworth, Southey and chums palpitating beneath their frock coats at the glories of the Lake District. Previously nature had been thought of as rather savage and nasty. The Romantics realised that this untamed landscape had its own kind of beauty. Later, Emily Brontë used the wildness of the Yorkshire moors as inspiration and embodiment of sexual passion in *Wuthering Heights*. A page or two of this makes Mills and Boon look feeble and today's pink-covered chicklit seem rather daft.

Despite appearances to the contrary, Alfred Wainwright was an incorrigible romantic. Underneath that padded anorak beat the heart of a passionate man. Much has been made of the emotional aridity of his first marriage but witness the prose inspired in the early books by his days and nights on his beloved hills and clearly this was a man who was sublimating his true feelings. However cold he was at home, he was in an ecstasy of longing and love on those hills. It sings through his descriptions of lofty peaks and dancing becks. Read the correspondence quoted in Hunter Davies' fine biography and you will see the same passion finding its expression in his letters to his second wife Betty. They are truly beautiful, intensely personal and reveal a very different man from the caricature of the harrumping sourpuss.

Germany boasts what it calls 'The Romantic Road'. It is, dispiritingly, a Tarmac highway from Wurzburg to Fussen in Bavaria and the south of the country. It was dubbed the *Romantische Straße* by travel agents in the 1950s to lure travellers along it with the promise of quintessentially German scenery. According to one motoring website, the most romantic road in Britain starts: 'In the regency town of Cheltenham (and) follows the path of sleepy towns and villages like Stow-on-the-Wold, Chipping Camden and Lower Slaughter and Upper Slaughter. And it really is romantic.'

Well, it may be *Top Gear*'s idea of romance but it's not mine. Get out of your BMW, get your Gore-Tex on and, as the young people say, get jiggy with it. Velcro fastenings are a boon by the way.

The Beautiful South

If you've ever been to the Grand Canyon, I'm willing to bet my 'Souvenir of Flagstaff' matching baseball cap and bumper sticker that you went to the South Rim. That's the way pretty much everyone does it; up the highway via the aforesaid Flagstaff from the big conurbations of the south-west USA like Phoenix and LA. For every visitor who peeks over this insane, vertiginous chasm from the North, a hundred clamber or ride down the Kaibab and Bright Angel trails of the South. The Canyon is only four miles across at its narrowest point, so from the crowded South Rim, the lonely northern edge seems near enough to touch, albeit across a vast, deep, mesmerising defile.

The reason for this discrepancy is all in the topography. The Canyon is a long lateral scar in the terrain. It may be only a few miles across, but it's nearly 300 miles long. By car, to get to the North Rim from the South involves a massive excursion, 215 miles or five hours and a climb of 1,000 feet or so. That's a long round trip, even in your gas-guzzling, air-conditioned Humvee with the Eagles playing. No wonder then that most of the rubberneckers and backpackers stay south.

In a minor way, the same applies to the Lake District. Most of the people who visit this lovely corner of England come from the south, from major urban centres like London, Manchester and Birmingham. For this reason, and for the more conventional prettiness of the landscape of the South Lakes, you will hardly find a day of the year when the gift shop tills and the pay and display machines of Bowness and Ambleside aren't ringing out in grateful exaltation. This is the trail I used to blaze myself when I first visited the area as a teenager. We'd chuck our tents and rods and primus stoves into Joe Mather's van on Fridays after school or college, hightail up the M6, breakfast at the transport café thingy in Ambleside (still there, gratifyingly) and have the tents pitched and the bumfluff shaved by the time the pubs of Hawkshead were open. There we'd drink all night, usually fail to pick up girls and wander unsteadily down to Esthwaite to fish for our breakfasts.

Hawkshead was a honeypot then and is even sweeter now. It's an easy target for walking purists' sneers; there are more knitwear outlets than gear shops and you'll find it easier to pick up a croissant here than a screw lock karabiner. But you can see why they come. It is lovely. And it's easy if you don't mind a bit of nose-to-nose traffic on the A591.

Down the road is Far Sawrey where the Beartrix Potter pilgrims come from Tokyo and Nagoya to 'coo' and smile and be unfailingly polite ordering lemonade in the pub. And then there's Tarn Hows, man-made of course (the purists will sneer again) but a heavenly if overcrowded place, and where John Hamersley and I caught 50 perch one idyllic summer's afternoon at the end of the 1970s.

Of course, if you do venture over Shap or Dunmail Raise, you'll find places and sights every bit as glorious. The Buttermere Valley may be the jewel in the Lakeland crown. There's Alfred Wainwright's favourite mountain: shaggy, gorgeous Haystacks. There are lonely tarns and high, bleak ridges. And if you do want creature comforts, Keswick is turning into Vegas-on-Derwent these days whilst my favourite restaurants in the whole of the Lake District are in Penrith and Great Salkeld.

But I'm not going to tell you which. I'd like to keep the North Lakes to myself for a while. There's a lot of The Beautiful South to explore, after all.

Hints and Glimpses

Once I got offered a lift by Lord David Owen. Well, when I say 'offered a lift', he wasn't driving. What I should have said is that I got offered the chance to spend an hour and a half in a car with Lord David Owen. For reasons that were nothing to do with the setting up of the SDP or UK foreign policy in the late 1970s, I declined.

I wasn't being rude to David – or Dave, as I'm sure by now I'd be calling him had we bonded in the back of the car. It was just that I quite fancied taking the train. The trip was from Edinburgh to Pitlochry where I was talking at a literary festival, and I quite fancied taking in the scenery.

Now there will be red-blooded, bearded walkers among you who find this a tad wimpy. Taking in the scenery will seem a rather weedy option if your idea of a relaxing day is swinging across Mickledore gripping a frayed rope between your teeth. But, even though I knew I wouldn't get a walk in, I wanted to tantalise myself with a glimpse and an idea.

Glimpses and hints are the stuff of walking to me. There are some walks I will do over and over, for reasons of comfort or practicality. I tramp up Bowscale Fell and over Moor Divock a lot. But I've never understood those men – it is nearly always men – who've climbed Helvellyn or Scafell or Buachaiile Etive Mor or Snowdon a hundred times and never wondered about that lonely hill over there or that curious looking forest on the map.

I can spend an hour or two in reverie, fantasy actually, with a glass of something nice to hand and before me a map of a region I know in my heart I'll never visit. I can look at the crowded contours of a rock face or a wooded valley and imagine the views and the silence and even the sunset. I'm not alone in this. Alfred Wainwright himself kept two sets of maps, one for the hill and one for the fireside and evening ruminations. I can take it to extremes. Recently I've been amusing myself with my new car's satnav facility and taking imaginary aerial journeys over the Padjelanta trail in Northern Sweden or the Tatra Mountains of Poland. Well, it beats typing in the co-ordinates for B&Q.

I made the trip to Pitlochry, by the way. The Firth of Forth was a roiling, heaving grey mass that looked wilder than the Baltic. The train squeezes between the sea and a steep wooded hill with a graveyard, a scene of gothic splendour and a wide crescent beach near Burntisland.

Just before Perth I noticed lonely hills and hollows ranging out through the mist and a couple of farmhouses clinging to sodden hills. Suddenly an arm of the sea rushes inland and beyond are some dense sylvan slopes rising in the murk. Then round the next bend, a huge ziggurat of a hill looms up, vast and purple with heather, and beyond that its neighbours range damp and dark and alluring. Driving the last few miles we pass Birnam Wood of *Macbeth* fame and The Hermitage where my local driver tells me I could see some of the tallest trees in Europe.

I probably won't see them though. Or climb that purple ziggurat of a hill or stroll along that crescent shore. It doesn't matter though. I might and I can. There are lots of tomorrows and lots of hints and glimpses and lots of real walks and wet feet still to come.

A Narrow Frame

I n one edition of that feisty samizdat hillzine *The Angry Corrie*, there's a report on Lancastrian Reg Baker's walk to the summit of Clougha Pike in the Trough of Bowland on June 23rd, 2007. As the piece points out, with the greatest respect the ascent of Clougha Pike isn't in the *Touching The Void* mould. It's a decent little bump but no Kanchenjuga, or even a Skiddaw come to that. No, what makes Reg's day out so noteworthy is that this was the 5,000th time he had climbed this particular hill.

This is, depending on your point of view, either rather charming or utterly nuts. Actually I think it's a bit of both and none the worse for that. Reg falls into one of three or maybe four general categories that have been posited to account for the monomaniac peak-bagger. He's a hillrunner, and Clougha is his local peak. In this way then, it's a kind of training circuit down at the gym. Except the views are better and you don't have to watch *Sky Sports News* or some moronic music channel that only seems to have Christina Aguilera videos.

Other categories of peak-bagger include professional guides and folk such as Craig Palmer, John Bennett, Nick Chetwood and Graham Restarick. All have been employed as professional felltop assessors by the Lake District National Park Weatherline to hike up Helvellyn every day to determine the conditions.

Every time this latter job comes up in conversation, there's usually a chorus of 'nice work if you can get it' and a general susurration of envious murmurs. I've never been so sure. If you have to do the ascent every day come rain or shine or hangover or man-flu, doesn't even such a glorious endeavour become as quotidian and routine as the office run? Eventually, don't even Sticks Ghyll and Swirral Edge assume the prosaic shape of the Aston Expressway or the Hangar Lane Gyratory System? Who can say but the gentlemen themselves.

What I can say is that although I'm a long, long way off 5,000 ascents of anything, I do fall into the category identified in the piece as ordinary walkers who end up doing the same walk again and again out of sheer convenience. I've had several old faves like this. Once every Christmas would see me up Sale Fell several times. Now, having changed my centre of Cumbrian gravity, it's more likely to be Great Mell Fell or Binsey or Dunmallard Hill over Ullswater.

Thinking about it, though, the hills I've probably roamed over most are the Clent Hills in Worcestershire, 15 minutes from my West Midlands base and the perfect Sunday afternoon or summer's evening stroll before a pint with friends in one of the little pubs that dot these gentle, very English hills.

Sometimes I get exasperated with my own lack of foresight or energy; usually when I'm pulling on my boots in the car park at Pooley Bridge for the umpteenth time. I think enviously of those who are even now walking the Ridgeway or the Pembrokeshire Coastal Path or Peru's Machu Picchu trail for the first time. Or gasping with wonder at a view never seen by human eyes before in some mountain vastness in Bhutan. I must have seen that 'No Fly Tipping' sign on Heughscar Hill a thousand times.

But there's a kind of pleasure too in getting to know a walk, letting the landscape become an old friend, learning to appreciate its quiet secrets and watching the seasons change across its features; seeing snow and rabbits and daffodils come and go, watching explosions of yellow and green fade to russet and black.

The great Cumbrian poet Norman Nicholson never moved from the house he was born in, in the small town of Millom. And yet his verse is as wise and rich and worldly as anyone's. Perhaps sometimes even a narrow frame can hold something to marvel at.

Strides and Sweat Patches

This may be the first and last time that the American avant-gard composer John Cage (born only a year or two after Alfred Wainwright but a very different kind of guy) gets mentioned here, but trust me, there is a reason. Cage's most notorious composition *4'33"* (Four minutes, thirty-three seconds) is also his most misunderstood. It's for any instrument and the idea is that the performer plays nothing for the duration of the piece. Many people thus take away the idea that the piece is four and a bit minutes of silence and is, therefore, a bit daft.

What Cage was actually trying to do was alert us to the fact that music, or at least sound, is all around us. The 'piece' then is the coughing of the audience, the bird song or sirens or train whistles heard in the distance, the thumping of our own pulse. And of course, it's a different piece every time.

In a similar vein, thinker and musician Brian Eno would make short tape recordings of the ambient sounds heard from his room and, after repeated re-hearings, would learn to appreciate these 'pieces' as music, to expect and anticipate certain sounds and noises and enjoy them almost as you would a chorus or middle eight, a baby crying, a car back-firing, the whistling of the paper boy.

What's this got to do with walking? Well, the other day I decided to walk to the pub. I'd been writing all day in my Lakes lair and decided that a brisk four miles down country lanes to my 'local' would set me up for a pint of Black Sheep and a low-cal, high-fibre feast of curry and chips. It's a route I've taken hundreds of times by car but I've never walked it before. The difference was a revelation.

For one, I saw things I've never seen. Little coppices and mysterious hollows and clearings in the woodland to the right, a fine crag formation in a nearby farmer's field, a lonely house with high windows up a hidden driveway. I'd passed these by often but always as a car passenger where, even at a conservative and law-abiding 30mph, such details are gone in a blink and a blur.

The journey even felt different. I could feel the shifts of gradients in my calves and my lungs. The distances began to take shape in my mind in a way they never had previously. A village that I'd always thought roughly halfway between my place and the pub in fact turned out to be much, much nearer the latter. When the journey takes six or seven minutes in air-conditioned containment, facts like that don't mean anything. But when the journey takes an hour and a quarter and is on foot, distance takes on new meanings as do every contour, vista and curve in the road.

It occurred to me that this is why we walk, to root ourselves in real human experience and real human scope. The internal combustion engine has had many benefits, it has brought friends and families and the cultural and geographical treasures of many nations closer. But it has also distorted our perspective of the world, made us lose sight (and sense, smell and touch) of the real physical world. Walking lets you know how the world really feels again, a world measured in strides and sweat patches. You literally get your feet back on the ground in a way that re-charges the batteries and re-aligns your view of the world to a healthier perspective.

And of course, the pint and the chips and the curry taste even better for the effort expended in getting to them.

Run for the Hills

More often than I'd care to be, I find myself sitting on a train criss-crossing Britain, watching the country – back gardens and sidings and village ponds – slide by at high speed. Hopefully at high speed, at least. I have come to know the West Coast Mainline like the back of my hand; and if it would be an exaggeration to say that it's become an old friend, certain stretches have nevertheless taken on a pleasing familiarity.

There are some beautiful and picturesque sections but none affects me quite as much as the right-hand vista seen when heading south between Shap and Lancaster. The poetry is probably lost on many; the long dark valley of Swindale has no lake, no crags, no signature summits. Some might even call it dreary; miles of empty, high ground, the odd forlorn track or clump of trees. But this, the emptiness and wildness, is what makes me sit up every time and think that however bad the weather outside, however pleasant the company or the hot bacon roll: 'I wish I was up there now.'

Cities have much to recommend them, much that I'd find hard to give up entirely. Clothes and record shops, restaurants, theatres. But increasingly often these days when I've had a few days in the country, on moors or mountains or in forests, and the time comes to return to 'civilisation', to car exhausts and queuing and Jeremy Kyle, that small voice inside me starts to say, 'Run... run for the hills and don't come back.'

Phillip Larkin, misanthropic as ever, wrote a verse about it called *Poetry of Departures* where he said:

Sometimes you hear, fifth-hand,
As epitaph:
He chucked up everything
And just cleared off,
And always the voice will sound
Certain you approve
This audacious, purifying,
Elemental move.

Lots of us do approve. Escape is a persistent fantasy. Some people fake elaborate demises, or pop out for a bottle of milk never to return until, five-stone lighter and shaggily bearded, they are discovered working as lumberjacks in Anchorage. I rarely consider anything so drastic but I imagine everyone reading this knows the appeal of disappearing 'far from the madding crowd,' as Thomas Hardy had it.

Willliam Blake put it a little differently: 'Great things are done when men and mountains meet. This is not done by jostling in the street.' For me, Blake has hit the nail on the head. Although you can find yourself in a Tesco-style queue on Striding Edge on August Bank Holiday Monday, you don't usually find yourself doing too much jostling when out in the wilds.

Savvy types have even tried to market this desire to 'get away from it all.' Skilfully placed adverts from the

Scottish Tourist Board on the Northern Line often show a picture of some ice-blue tarn or snowy peak along with a tantalising strapline like, 'Don't you wish you were here?'; implying but leaving unsaid, 'And not stuck with a massive student backpack jammed in your face or rammed up against a sweaty armpit.'

There's even a TV show catering to this fantasy, although *Escape to the Country* seems to be more about making a killing on your flat in Streatham and moving to Tunbridge Wells, than living off rancid yak butter tea with nomads on the Mongolian Steppes.

In the end maybe we want the safety net of coming back, to microwaves and plasma screens and such. But while we are out there, the wilderness is a balm and solace and battery charger. And when we return to home and hearth and mortgages, we might open the map or guidebook and find a stray blade of grass, reminding us that we were once a free man or woman in the hills.

The Allure of Risk

As previously quoted, the great English mystic, radical and visionary William Blake once said: 'Great things are done when men and mountains meet. This is not done by jostling in the street.' Blake was far more likely to be seen in frock coat and breeches than Gore-Tex and The North Face but he clearly knew something about the appeal of high places.

Writing this has made me become very aware that I should not assume that we are all hillwalkers. Yes, it was hills that drew me away from the fireside, the restaurant and the pub when I first began walking earnestly as a 20-something music hack in the late 80s. And as long as the legs hold out, I'll be climbing hills.

But the older I get the more I've come to appreciate the charms of other terrains and other forms of walking: beaches, woods, coastal paths, moors. During the bleak days of foot and mouth, I enjoyed town trails through Ludlow and Bridgnorth and acquired a habit that persists. But all the time there was a vague hankering after the solitude of mountains.

Mountains are elevated places, both literally and metaphorically. That they stand aloof and remote makes them special. The very fact that attaining their summits takes effort and takes you away from the crowds (unless it's Helvellyn on Bank Holiday Monday) makes them places of pilgrimage and often awe.

I don't really understand the slightly macho world of the climber. It's the places and their ambience that lure me, rather than endurance or competitiveness. But I once interviewed legendary mountaineer Doug Scott and he told me of the trancelike state he'd arrived at after his ascent of the Carstensz Pyramid in Indonesia and I could understand what he meant when he talked of an exhaustion so total that he lay for hours in his tent, 'watching my own thoughts drift by in front of me, so slowly that I could reach out and grab them as they passed.'

Then of course there is danger. Climbers always insist that it is not the risk that attracts them, that in fact it is all about minimising it and that only a fool courts disaster. They may think they mean it too. But clearly the sense of life lived literally on the edge and the bracing, almost exhilarating nearness of death is something that the Scotts, Simpsons and Hastons of this world crave or craved.

I like my dram afterwards and living to tell the tale. But even I know something of the allure of risk. Once, having badly underestimated the length of the ascent, I stood and looked at the length of the Buttermere High Stile ridge, noted the fast approaching dusk and my complete lack of light or shelter and realised that if I didn't start to move fast, putting several miles and a tricky descent under my belt in the next hour or so, I might be spending the night on the mountain. If not worse.

The sensation I felt was fear. But I know that there was a kind of thrill mixed in there too. Let's not fall into the trap of seeing mountains as scary, though, or something to be 'conquered'. You will never conquer them. Treat them with respect, though, and you will make friends for life of them. You can find a cure to most of life's ills up there. As John Muir wrote: 'Climb the mountains and get their good tidings. Nature's peace will flow into you as sunshine flows into trees. The winds will blow their own freshness into you, and the storms their energy, while cares will drop off like autumn leaves.'

Land Art

O n my bookshelf at home, I have a postcard bought a few years ago from Tate Modern that gives me as much pleasure as any piece of art I have ever encountered. But I know that it mystifies as many people as it delights and that when people ask me what it is and why I like it, they wonder what on earth I see in this 40-year-old black and white picture of a daisy-filled meadow with a cross shape depicted on the grass by the judicious removal of daisy heads.

The work is called *England, 1968* and is by the Bristolian artist Richard Long. Something about its quiet beauty, its sense of a very specific place and time now gone, and the knowledge that the 'sculplture' of the dead-headed daisies is transient, makes it a powerful piece for me, much more so – and I say this with the greatest respect for other people's taste – than the more conventional prettiness of Constable or Turner.

It's maybe no surprise that Richard Long is a favourite of Bill Drummond, the pop musician and thinker perhaps most famous for burning a million pounds. Drummond once cut a Richard Long original into 20,000 fragments and sold them for a pound each, in what was either a wry and provocative comment about the worth of art or a piece of philistine madness, depending on your point of view.

Land art has been a contentious but busy genre of the art world for several decades now. One of the most ambitious and celebrated examples is Robert Smithson's *Spiral Jetty* (1970), at Rozel Point, Great Salt Lake, Utah.

Smithson built a spiral pier of basalt, limestone and earth extending over a mile from the shore. Wind, waves and erosion mean that the piece was doomed and this was just as Smithson intended.

The work was destroyed having been seen by almost no one. And this was sort of the point, I think. The obscurity and impermanence of the piece added to its richness, just like the sense of privilege you get when you see a virgin snowfield on a fellside or a fabulous sunset from a vantage point you know that no one else is sharing.

Perhaps the best modern example of such art is in the work of Andy Goldsworthy. His stone cones placed in isolated places are meant to accrue moss, dirt and weeds and his ice sculptures are destroyed by the very thing – brilliant sunshine – that illuminates them and shows them to their best advantage.

Anthony Gormley isn't a land artist as such but his installations such as the profoundly moving *Another Place* – a host of silent figures walking out to sea from the Merseyside coast – work on us because of their relationship to the landscape around them. They would not work if shown in a gallery.

There will always be those who dismiss such work as 'pretentious'. I don't agree. Art's job is to mystify and baffle much more than it is to amuse and reassure. When I see the work of Long or Gormley or Goldsworthy, I get the same feeling that I do when I walk in the wilderness at twilight, when I wild camp, when I find a quiet corner of a river or hill. Not a feeling of safety or comfort but of awe, a feeling that the world is stranger and more beautiful than we can imagine.

Which is why some people picnic in a lay-by with a copy of the *Daily Mail* and you and I, reader, go out in the rain and mist and get blissfully lost. I'll never get to see *Spiral Jetty* now and neither will you. Perhaps that is what makes it so special.

Salad Cream

Some years ago, someone at Heinz, it of 57 varieties fame, noticed that one of its varieties, namely salad cream, was not doing so well anymore. Balsamic vinegar, mayonnaise and a new health consciousness had made this Sunday teatime staple – best enjoyed with a spring onion, chunk of mature cheddar, tin of salmon and the chart rundown with Simon Bates – seem old fashioned and downmarket. So the marketing men came up with a brilliant wheeze. They announced that production of the tangy viscous condiment was to cease. Cue acres of coverage, mass public outcry and an overnight doubling of sales.

All of which is a long-winded way of saying that you often take life's little pleasures for granted until they threaten to disappear. And it applies to the freedom to roam as much as anything else. The most obvious recent example of this was the foot and mouth outbreak of 2001. I remember vividly coming down off the hill after a day wandering the lonely 'Back o'Skiddaw' like Great Calva and Bakestall. We descended by Whitewater Dash Falls and as we climbed the stile by Peter House Farm, a farmer got down from his tractor and put up a sign on the stile saying that, because of foot and mouth and government legislation, the track and surrounding fells would be out of bounds until further notice.

I remember looking longingly up the valley to the twisted ribbon of white that is the waterfall and feeling a sensation rather like a door closing or curtain coming down. It was a gloomy feeling and I hoped that this enforced separation wouldn't last long. The melancholy mood would have been made much, much worse had I known that afternoon would be the last time I would set foot on the fells or indeed pretty much any open country for months to come.

As Joni Mitchell sang, 'you don't know what you've got 'til it's gone,' and that can apply to even the most devoted walker and those of us who think we will never take the beauty of the open places for granted.

These musings were prompted by my knee. While sojourning in a remote Lake District valley, I decided to dash up a small but good-looking fell called the Nab, which incidentally was for many years out of bounds itself as a private deer reserve until the coming of the right to roam legislation.

It was a dash too; a quick up and down between the showers just to get a bit of exercise and my dose of the fells. Somewhere along the line, though, I managed to twist my knee and limped through the following months in varying degrees of pain. The physical ache wasn't as onerous, though, as the sense of the fells being out of bounds.

Even the shortest walks were difficult and so I made do with twilight strolls or parking up in various vantage points and looking longingly at the mist on High Pike or the rain coming down on the bald pate of Great Mell Fell. The weather didn't help either. The complete lack of a summer that year brought its own restrictions.

Walking is all about freedom, particularly when you walk in high places. Anything that curtails that freedom – legal, medical or meteorological – is a pain to be endured and railed against. But if any of these things do have a positive side, it's that they remind us not to take the glories of the countryside and our freedom to explore it for granted. Right, anyone know anything about knees?

A Nice Leg-Stretcher

Some names are almost guaranteed to get an emotional response from the average British soul; Thatcher, say, or Maradona, or Diana. You can add to that list the name of a certain chemical industrialist called Beeching. Just the other week I listened to various British people spit out his name with varying degrees of venom. A mild-mannered retired teacher quivered with rage on Piccadilly Station as he told me that, 'That man was a blight on the British way of life. He did more damage with a pen than the Luftwaffe did with their bombs.'

What Beeching did, back in 1963, was close down a third of the British railway network, a decision of monumental short-sightedness and arrogance whose effects are still felt today in stressed commuters, gridlocked roads, pollution, and towns and villages left high and dry.

I've made a TV programme about him and it was hard to find anyone who didn't view him as a callous bogeyman. But standing on the station at Rose Hill in Marple, a useless spur of track that Beeching somehow thought should survive (there is another perfectly good station in Marple with trains going the same way), a defence of Doctor B did start to formulate.

At the end of the platform you can see where Beeching's axe fell; the tracks just stop, the way is blocked and trees grow over the former line. And beyond that stretches the Middlewood Way; a ten-mile 'linear park' between Macclesfield and Rose Hill that was opened on May 30th, 1985 by cheery, hirsute botanist Doctor David Bellamy.

It follows the route of the old railway and though no trains run these days, the line is still busy with walkers, dog walkers, cyclists, joggers and horse riders. It passes beneath a variety of railway architecture and if you take your *Observer* book, you can spot all kinds of bird and plantlife.

Walking along old railway tracks has much to recommend it. There's a certain nostalgic charm, a hint of poignancy and, on a practical level, the routes are usually pretty flat – if often long – and thus suitable for those with limited mobility or when the tops are wreathed in clag. The downside is that the environs are often interesting or pleasant rather than spectacular, although that said, the scenery on the Keswick Railway Path is obviously superb.

This four-mile-long footpath was created from a section of the old Keswick to Cockermouth route, still the subject of controversy. A campaign to reopen it is ongoing and it's hard to see what Beeching was thinking when he closed a route with such obvious tourist potential yet left Rose Hill open, a ghost station that's a gloomy living museum. Still, it's an ill wind and all that, and when ill winds mean that more adventurous stuff is off the agenda, the Keswick Railway Footpath is a nice leg-stretcher and suitable for almost everyone. My mother-in-law did it in her disability scooter, although she did get a bit nervous where a specially constructed walkway passes over one of the gorges of the River Greta. That's the best bit, by the way.

There's more to be found about railway walking in Hunter Davies' fine book, *Walking the Tracks*. And if you want to hear a lovely, sad song about Beeching's follies, listen to 'The Slow Train' by Flanders and Swann. As many of these old lines have had Tesco and the like built on them, they can never be reopened. In which case, maybe more of them can be used for the benefit of walkers and we can find a few good words for the bad doctor.

Money Well Spent

As I write these words, a red squirrel called Ted is diligently and skilfully munching his way into a hazelnut on the veranda about eight feet away from me. We like to think of him as 'Ted', although that's increasingly becoming a generic term for what we think might be as many as four of them who come every day from dawn to dusk to my Cumbrian garden.

They are, frankly, spoiled rotten. The ready-made squirrel mix from the Birds Bistro down the road is no longer tasty or alluring enough for them and they've even started to turn their cute noses up at the Italian hazelnuts. So it's the American ones, which are only marginally less expensive than truffles and foie gras.

Credit crunch or no credit crunch, this is one economy I won't be making any time soon. Like the blessed Alfred Wainwright himself, I'm pretty ambivalent about wildlife when I'm out and about on my walks. I can spend 20 minutes peering over a stile at the private parts of cattle in an attempt to ascertain their sex and therefore whether I can cross a field unmolested.

Whereas others see goats and think of *The Sound of Music* and billy goats from picture books, I assume they'll butt me, eat my sandwiches – famously the ones at Low Water under Coniston will do both – and I generally conclude that the Jamaicans have it about right when they turn goats into curry. I am ambivalent about sheep and I can't tell a finch from a tit… or maybe even an osprey.

But something about the red squirrel enchants me. Maybe it's the poignancy of what Hollywood would call the back story; our native shy English resident with its echoes of Beatrix Potter and the Tufty Club driven out by larger, bolder, less charming US invaders. (I wouldn't dream of it but I'm surprised more politically inclined liberal wildlife fans haven't tried to make more of this metaphor).

The US-imported greys, imported of course by stupid humans without a thought to the ecological balance of these islands, give the reds a disease called parapox to which they themselves are immune. If you have ever seen a red with parapox, it will break your heart and give you another reason to cherish them.

I know too that the reds will go soon. I hope differently and as I write this a Red Squirrel Conservation Week is in full swing and I commend this wholeheartedly. Maybe we can turn the tide. But the gloomy realist in me thinks that our grandchildren won't see red squirrels outside of places like Formby Reserve which are, essentially, zoos. When people say that we should preserve things for our grandchildren I'm fairly unmoved anyway. If the grandkids are anything like their grandparents, they don't deserve it and will set about ruining it with the same short-sightedness and greed that their forebears did.

So as the world's economies continue their slide into chaos and the average Joe like me and you pays dearly for the incompetence of super-rich bankers, a few quid for Ted's favourite treats feels like money well spent to me.

There are some things you can't put a price on. And one of them is that flash of russet on a summer's morning or in the dusk of an autumn forest, once seen, never forgotten.

Red Letter Day

Great Mell Fell is an odd, amiable, lopsided pudding of a hill in the north-eastern corner of the Lake District. With its dome-like forehead and sparse Bobby Charlton comb-over of fir and larch, it bears a striking resemblance to a radio producer of my acquaintance who shall be nameless, though I always think of it as ------- -------- Fell. And, no, I'm not telling. Standing slightly aloof or maybe spurned by its beefy chums, it's a familiar landmark to those speeding by along the A66, the first of the Lake District fells if you're coming from the east and the motorway.

Great Mell Fell is probably no-one's idea of a forbidding summit. It's no Annapurna, no K2, no Eiger. It's not even a Catbells really. The first time I tried it I did get lost and turn back but that's simply because of an unfortunate combination of a really misleading old National Trust sign and a rare lack of clarity by the Blessed AW (Alfred Wainwright). Anyway, I climbed it again for maybe the fourth time and this particular time it really meant something. It was a red letter day, a summit that called for champagne and kisses and a nicely triumphant walk back to the car.

The reason was that Great Mell Fell was the first fellwalk my wife had been able to manage in over a year. Polymyalgia, a rheumatic condition, undiagnosed at first, made serious walking of any kind agonising for her. Fells had given way to short flat strolls and even they had become arduous. She didn't want to say it, or even think it, and I wasn't going to let her, but the nagging doubt remained that she'd have to say goodbye at least to the fells which she loves and we've discovered together.

Fortunately, with the help of steroids, things had been on the mend and, with all the usual provisos about 'turning back any time we wanted' and 'just enjoying being out', we set out from the Matterdale road with poles and rucksacks. These should be the things you say to yourself on any walk, the common sense walker's mantras that stop you overstretching yourself and getting exposure on a Pennine bog or clinging to Sharp Edge by your fingernails. This time though, it did feel important to get to that cairn, to have that traditional Twix and Thermos, to take in the best view of Blencathra around. The aforementioned Alfred Wainwright says in the conclusion to his *Western Fells* volume that he was lucky never to have sustained an accident during his travels and researches as 'a broken leg would have meant a broken heart.'

I mention this because it occurred to me that many people reading this might be anxious about their walking future through illness or injury or other circumstance. Well, don't be. The simple pleasure of putting one foot in front of another – or one wheel or stick maybe – in the glorious outdoors is something that remains do-able by nearly all of us. The time will come when none of us, however burly and bearded or wiry and whippet-like is going to 'top out' on Helvellyn again. But when that day comes there'll be photos and films and blisters and maps and friends to remind us. And we'll find different

Helvellyns, be they Great Mell Fell or our local country park or canal towpath. AW was wrong this time. A broken leg doesn't have to mean a broken heart. But it may mean that you have to change your horizons and perspectives for a while. It doesn't matter. The hills and rivers and woods will wait for you.

Guilty As Charged

Standing with the young farmer on a field in his land up at High Wray in the South Lakes, I was looking out admiringly on the view from his 'back garden', a vista stretching out across Windermere to the Fairfield Horseshoe, Red Screes and Caudale Moor. 'What's that?' I asked, noticing a large, shapely body of water nestling below us in a fold of the hills. 'It looks very familiar.'

'Blelham Tarn,' he said and of course the memories came flooding back; summer's evenings walking the shore with mates en route from campsite to the Drunken Duck or Outgate Inn – the tarn lovely and still and, for us teenage fishermen, tantalisingly unobtainable for the most part because of restrictions imposed by Windermere Anglers and the Freshwater Biological Association, it being a richly fertile scientific jewel.

I knew that I knew it; just as you never forget an old friend's face. Because at the risk of being soppy (and if you aren't a tad romantic, I doubt if you're reading this or enjoy beautiful countryside) Blelham Tarn was an old friend; shy, beautiful, much-loved and fondly remembered.

Some people baulk at this kind of 'anthropomorphising' of the landscape and to a degree I share their reservations. Part of the bracing thrill of being in the high places that I like, or on a wild and lonely moor, is the austere inhumanity of them. They are stern but neither are they fickle; they exist outside of the human dimension of change and decay. They are eternal and immutable. Or at least they aren't going to change much until the next ice age or geological upheaval.

But landscape can become a friend and can take on human qualities, or at least living ones. Famously, walker and author Alfred Wainwright described Haystacks, his favourite fell and final resting place, as standing 'unabashed and unashamed in the midst of a circle of much loftier fells, like a shaggy terrier in the company of foxhounds.' And, speaking of a prominent, bulbous boulder on another summit, he remarks a tad ungallantly that, 'some women have faces like that.' More generously, after a night awake on the fells when he admits to being scared of the dark and gets through the still dark hours by chain-smoking, he talks of his relief and pleasure at seeing the outlines of the fells, 'old friends' emerging in the roseate dawn.

That's how I feel about my favourite hills. If it's wrong to ascribe them personalities then I'm afraid I'm guilty as charged. Skiddaw is big and friendly, a gentle giant, but one that you wouldn't want to get on the wrong side of. Helvellyn is haughty and has let its huge popularity make it a little conceited, a supermodel of a fell. Blencathra is imperious, beautiful and somewhat forbidding. Loughrigg Fell is playful and cheery.

In fact, my wife and I have taken this to an absurd extreme in the case of one of our favourite haunts, Great Mell Fell. As mentioned earlier, its sloping bald pate dotted with a thin comb-over cum tonsure of trees make it a dead ringer for a certain famous radio producer and executive of my acquaintance. So much so in fact that we actually call it after him now rather than Great Mell Fell. 'Look, there's snow on…'

Ah, but that would be telling. And you never know I may still need a job from him one day. So let's draw a veil over that and leave you instead with this thought: Clough Head. Aloof, awkward to get to grips with, but always something interesting going on. It's got to be named after Brian, hasn't it?

Stolen Moments

Don't tell anyone I said so but isn't stealing great? Not your actual light-fingered theft of course but 'stealing' in the sense of purloined pleasures, treats taken guiltily when backs are turned. Do you remember that delicious forbidden frisson when, in junior school, the big TV on its ludicrous metal gantry was wheeled in for *Fun with Maths* or *Words and Pictures* and you would get a moment or two of, gasp, normal, naughty 'fun' TV before the broadcast (probably *Farmhouse Kitchen* or Jack Scott doing the weather). And can there be any doubt that the greatest chip of all (as Whitney Houston so nearly sang) is never your own, but the one nabbed furtively from someone else's tray or plate?

These thoughts came to mind one day when, mooching about somewhere on a frosty Kirkstone Pass between Red Screes and John Bell's Banner, I thought, 'What a lovely thing to be doing on a Friday lunchtime.' I hope you know what I mean. Walking is a delight at any time but we tend to fit these things in where we can around the daily routine: holidays, weekends, evenings. That's why Striding Edge and the Old Man of Coniston are more crowded than the Ikea checkout on a Bank Holiday Monday. Even with changing work patterns and supposed 24/7 living, most of us still head for the hills and dales and moors outside the demands of the 9 to 5.

In the wonderful poem *Toads Revisited* by the equally wonderful if lugubrious Philip Larkin, he wanders a park in Hull on a mid-week afternoon and speculates on the people he sees. Things are different now but back the in the 1960s it was probably right of Larkin to conclude that they were a melancholy lot, misfits and outpatients and those generally left behind by life, convincing him that in the end it's probably better to have something constructive if dull to do with one's days, and let 'the toad work squat on my life' as he once said.

I'm with him up to a point. But only to a point. These past few years I've written a couple of English travel books which have involved what might be laughingly called 'research' entailing often strolling through country parks and village greens and market squares in the middle of the working week. And it was great. Feeding ducks with sprightly pensioners or browsing the stalls with off-duty young mums. The sense that really I should be sitting at a desk somewhere just heightened the pleasure.

I opened a school extension in Patterdale where huge picture windows give the kids glorious floor-to-ceiling views of Oxford Crag and Place Fell as they work. Utterly lovely; but I couldn't help but sympathize with the teachers who must have to look enviously at the truanting, the holidaying, the early retired or the absconding walkers who amble smiling by as they make their way to Angle Tarn and High Street.

Anyway, back to Kirkstone Pass and as walks go, it was nothing, a quick mooch out of the car really. But that wasn't the point. The beauty lay in the stealing of an hour or two of freedom, the theft of time that by right should belong to desk or duty, kitchen or kids or workbench. This isn't irresponsibility – just one of the little adventures of being alive.

By the time you read this I am hoping to be well into my New Year's resolution which is to steal more of these hours. Three or four evenings a week I spend in a radio studio in Manchester and as jobs go, few could be less onerous or more fun. But I still intend to keep a pair of boots and a map in a desk drawer and, when the whim and the weather take me, get out into the surrounding countryside. So if one of these bright afternoons, you meet me on Winter Hill or Rivington Pike or Dovestone Reservoir....you didn't see me, right?

Boot Biography

At the risk of making this a contender for 'dullest opening sentence of the year,' I bought a new pair of boots the other day. To a non-walker, this transaction must seem hardly worthy of comment. But I fancy everyone reading these words will know what a significant hour the acquisition of new walking boots is. It's more than just a matter of new footwear; it's a rite of passage and a pause for reflection.

TS Eliot's Prufrock may have 'measured out his life in coffee spoons,' but walkers can calibrate and recall their seasons on the hills, moors, towpaths and country lanes via their old boots. My new Black Raichles (rather sexy in a menacing *Where Eagles Dare* way, I think) have taken their place as 'best boots' which means that my battered old Zamberlans are now 'reserve boots'. These have served me well for at least a decade, probably more.

I can't remember prosaic things like dates but I do remember that the first day I bought them, I gave my previous favourites (a rather snazzy pair of North Face Gore-Tex in the old Burnley/West Ham/Aston Villa colours) to my friend John and we both got acquainted on a round of the Northern Fells on a frozen, azure day in December; five fells, a flask at Trusmadoor and a long, happy trudge down the old Roman road to Longlands – one of those glorious days that lives long in the memory.

The Zamberlans have been good to me and, though it sounds absurd and clichéd, have become like old friends. I have got to know the foibles and idiosyncrasies of their lacings. I know exactly what depth and flow of bog or river will cause them to leak gently. The little diagonal slash on the right instep was gained when vaulting a barbed wire fence in Ennerdale. These boots have been to the bottom of the Grand Canyon and the top of Scafell Pike. I wish them a long and happy semi-retirement on the gentler slopes of Clent and the Malverns.

Of course, another good reason why the purchase of new walking boots is no trivial matter is that nowadays it involves a goodly amount of justifiable palaver. Once, the Whympers and the Wainwrights, our pioneering antecedents, would take to the high places in old football boots plastered with 'clinkers', or wellies or such. Josh Naylor, the hardy shepherd of Wasdale, probably still does the Bob Graham round in his bedroom slippers.

I like to be well shod, though; which is why the day after Boxing Day you could find me tramping up a bijou artificial stone slope in a famous Keswick outdoor gear shop whilst a nice young woman talked to me about insoles. I repeat; this is justifiable palaver. A few years ago, I was having such agonies on descent that I really thought my fellwalking days were behind me. Intelligent staff at that same shop – and a smart physio – told me that the problem was my curious gait, left uncorrected for years. A pair of decent insoles later, the problem vanished. Trust me, they aren't a gimmick.

But this is the practical stuff. Old boots, like much old favourite gear, take on a patina and a history that causes us to reflect on the passing of time, on the past and hopefully the future. When I see the creases in my Ordnance Survey maps and the massive tea stain on my *Northern Fells* Wainright (acquired in a gale on the slopes of Bakestall) it prompts a little reverie. In the same way, as I slip into my shiny new boots, I wonder how long it will take for the shine to fade, and what nicks and scratches these will accrue, and how many more pairs of boots I'm destined to get through before the walking's over.

Plenty I hope. And I wish you the same.

Highs and Lows

'The higher you go, the better the kind of person you meet.' Now normally this isn't the kind of sentiment I'd have any time for; snobbish and aloof you might say. But the speaker, a Lake District sheep farmer called Eric I met, wasn't talking about social climbing but actual climbing, not rungs of the class ladder but feet and metres of hillside.

Let me be clear about what he meant and also I hope dispel any hint of macho, beardy posturing. Fell and hillwalking is merely one kind of pedal activity and there's nothing intrinsically superior about it. Some people have no interest whatsoever in gradients and ascents and why should they?

I love the hills but I also love forests, country lanes, towpaths, town trails, anything that gets me putting one foot after another and leaving behind the head jangle of modern life. But what Eric was specifically referring to were the walkers who visit his valley, Great Langdale, the ones who cross his fields, gates and walls.

It's a generalisation but I think I know, ahem, 'where he's coming from.' What he meant is that it's the casual visitor, the one who doesn't stray far from the car park and the beer garden who tends to give him the most headaches, be it litter or minor vandalism or whatever. On the morning I spent with Eric and his family, I saw first-hand the crisp bags and empty plastic water bottles left discarded by the path and the breathtaking arrogance of the dog owners who let their pets run wild off leads amongst herds of

Herdwicks. Eric loses 40 sheep a year, chased off crags or into ravines, gullies and tarns, because of dogs; or rather because of their owners since Fido is merely doing what nature intended and can't be blamed for human stupidity and rudeness.

So what Eric meant was that the higher up the paths and fells you climb, so the crowds thin out and the people you encounter tend to be connoisseurs, if you like, the ones who were most appreciative of the landscape and prepared to seek out its hidden delights. It's a view that was shared by William Blake when he said, 'Great things are done when men and mountains meet. This is not done by jostling in the street.' To put it another way, the damage to Eric's drystone walls was practically all confined to the valley bottom. And if all this sounds a bit 'heightist' then it may be better to say that it's probably the person you find deeper in the wood or in the most obscure corners of the dale who value the landscape most.

Be honest. As walkers we like to think we're a cut above. Compared to devotees of other pastimes – darts, maybe, or monster truck racing – the image of walkers is genteel, perhaps even a little conservative. We close gates, we nibble Kendal Mint Cake, we take our litter home with us. Above all we appreciate the countryside where we take our enjoyment and we can be a little sneering towards those who take their pleasure elsewhere, in Blackpool or Bluewater say.

But don't we have our Blackpools too? I no more understand the folks who stand in line to go over Striding Edge on a Bank Holiday Monday or follow the crowds up the eroded trail to the summit of the Old Man of Coniston than I do the ones who queue for the rides at the pleasure beach. And just because it's an Evian bottle or an organic granola energy bar wrapper, it's no better than a can of Badger Bitter or a packet of Dairylea Dunkers. Left behind for Eric to pick up, it's still rubbish.

Talk to people like Eric and it becomes quickly apparent that like every other large group of people, we have our selfish, thoughtless element. We have the ones who don't think that rules or guidelines apply to them, the ones who leave Tango cans on cairns or ring the mountain rescue because they realise that they're going to be late for the table they've booked back in the village. Eric compared it to football crowds: 'You get 40,000 people at a match and the vast majority are well-behaved, reasonable people. But in that amount of people you will always get a few bad 'uns.' Let's hope he never means us.

Away From It All...

I write these words in the warm early evening sunshine at the end of one of the major public holidays of the year. I am in my very favourite place in the world, the English Lake District, and I have spent the day happily wandering the hills hereabouts. Not so many miles away, in the fleshpots of Keswick, Grasmere and Bowness, there will have been throngs and crowds comparable to Oxford Street in December or Birmingham's Broad Street on a Saturday night.

The difference with the latter is that whereas in the bars of Brum the competition is to see who can wear the least – girls in dresses like handkerchiefs and lads in T-shirts – in Keswick and Ambleside, there will have been anoraks in profusion; layer upon wicking layer of Gore-Tex and wool, and clacking phalanxes of walking poles vital for the arduous ascent of the craft shop stairs or the chippie.

It is easy to be cynical about the Lake District. It is, in some ways, the Cheryl Cole or Mylene Klass of our natural landscape; pretty but ubiquitous, over-exposed and a little obvious for some. They will prefer the Northumberlands and Ochils, the Bjorks and the Tori Amoses if you will; quirkier, worthier, more awkward to access. It's not an analogy that's going to hold up for very long, though, I grant you.

From another perspective, the Lakes mini-industry has a somewhat inflated notion of its own importance. The shrewish Caledonian wits at *The Angry Corrie* hillzine dismiss it as the 'Ponds District', a reference to the fact that, compared to the huge and imperious lochs of the Highlands, the Lake District's Ullswater, Ennerdale and Buttermere are but tiddlers.

But what tiddlers! From Wordsworth to Auden, Kurt Schwitters to Ken Russell, Hunter to Melvyn, those of us who write and talk and paint and film and stuff have written and talked and painted and filmed this most beautiful corner of Britain. There. I've said it. And I make no apologies. We should be partisan about the things we love. I love the Worcestershire hills on a late summer evening with friends and the promise of a beer at the Bell and Cross in Belbroughton. I love the almost serene upland tracts of the Brecon Beacons. I love the brooding grim solemnity of the West Pennine Moors on a winter's dusk. But nothing quite makes me catch my breath like the Lake District.

It has been having this effect for a century and a half, since the first Victorian tourists came and reached for their smelling salts and nosegays when confronted with the raw, primal landscape of water and crag, scree and moor. They found it exhilarating but savage, so much so that they would only view it with their backs to it, the scenery framed and tamed by tiny portable looking glasses, shrunken to the dimensions of a bijou cameo.

From this quaint habit comes the equally quaint term 'picturesque'. It's easy to sneer at this miniaturised notion of beauty and splendour but, in truth, compactness is perhaps the Lake District's great virtue. Lakeland is not alone in having elegant waters, lonely hills, big, braw mountains, sparkling falls and eerie forests. But nowhere else has them in such concentration. By infernal combustion engine, you can get from one end of it to the other in an hour, except perhaps on a Bank Holiday when the cars crawl bumper to bumper through Windermere and groan over Honister and Wrynose.

Which brings me back to today. I spent this Bank Holiday, the one now ending in a hazy, unseasonably warm sunset, attaining the summit of High Pike from the hamlet of Fellside via the steep, scarred ghylls and abandoned mines of Roughton and Short Grain and the hause from Hare Shaw. I had the wind shelter to myself and shared the summit with a handful of nice folk getting 'away from it all'. I imagine the crowds were 12-deep on Helvellyn.

I love the fact that you can still find those spots even here in the most beautiful corner of England. There. I've said it again. And I have to admit that even when you can't find them, I'm partial to the occasional fleshpot myself.

Oases of Calm

I came across it unexpectedly, having made my way on the raised duckboards through the sluggish pools of the wetlands, then striding out across the heath behind Stenner Woods and over the wilds.

Suddenly, there it was, shining and fast-flowing in the spring sun, eddies and pools whirling around little rocky islets. I followed the curve of the river along its high-sided banks, ravines almost, until another noise made itself heard above the hubbub of the waters; less pleasant, more insistent. Finally, when I reached the hard shoulder of the M62 and could smell the fumes of the lorries bound for Liverpool, I gave up and headed back to the dark recesses of the wood. I walked across the oozing wetlands again, through the weird, dense vegetation. It was all positively Mesozoic. If you ignored the nearby maisonettes.

Fletcher Moss is not a moss, it's a man. He (that's Alderman Fletcher Moss) was an eccentric Mancunian official who has now given his name to the 21 acres of gardens and open spaces that border the Millgate fields, the Stenner Woods and the flood plain of the Mersey and that sit conveniently and rather oddly in the heart of suburban Didsbury.

At New Year I made a sort of resolution that, even during my city life, generally in the cities of Birmingham or Manchester, I would get 'away from it all'. It wasn't just for exercise. You can get the lungs and legs going by pounding the pavements of the new Bullring Centre or Deansgate. But: a) you can too easily be tempted by the

Apple Store, Waterstones or, let's face it, Greggs; and b) you don't get that head-clearing sense of space and peace and different horizons without some running water, wind, birdsong, grass and trees.

Or at least I don't. Which is why this year has seen me exploring the little oases of countryside, the unexpected flowerings of natural landscape that lurk and luxuriate in even our biggest, most crowded urban sprawls. Take the Sandwell and Woodgate Valley country parks. Both are within a few miles of the centre of Brum. And in truth, the cafés and gifty bits are full of kids and dogs and buggies on any decent Sunday. But let's not be snobbish. To see working class urban folk enjoying fresh air and picnic tables is gladdening when they could be slumped slack-jawed in front of one of Simon Cowell's depressingly ubiquitous, soulless offerings.

And you don't have to go far from the visitor centre to leave the barking and the ringtones behind and be lulled instead by the sound of winds through grasses, birdsong, horses and the susurrations of water. In the case of Sandwell Valley these are two pretty, shy sheets called the Ice Pool and the Cascade Pool, relics from the days when this was a Benedictine Priory founded by William Fitz-Ansculf in the 1100s and surviving until Henry VIII's purge of the monasteries in the 16th century. All this is a prawn sandwich's throw from West Brom's ground at the Hawthorns.

Of course there are drawbacks. You do come across a lot of men and women from the council in high-vis tabards making a hell of a racket with leaf blowers and power saws. You don't get that on Schiehallion or Scafell. But they're only doing their job and a good job it is too, keeping these little wildernesses tame enough for city folk to enjoy in lunch hours and Sunday mornings, when hills and moors may be out of reach, but the stout shoes or trainers are lying in the car boot and the forecast is good and you can't face another minute of Simon Cowell.

Winter of
Discontent

On the edge of the West Pennine Moors above the Lancashire town of Bolton, just where Coal Pit Road (coming up from the farm teashop where they do a mean rhubarb crumble ice cream, by the way) meets the open moor and the track to Winter Hill, there's a plaque set in an imposing stone by the path. The first line reads 'Will You Come O'Sunday Morning?' taken from the song by the local writer Allan Clark. The lines are an invitation to take to the moors and leave behind the rattle of the looms and the workaday concerns of the town.

That is exactly what generations of working people everywhere have done, but particularly in the north and sometimes despite the best, or should that be worst, efforts of landowners and the authorities. Indeed what this fine stone commemorates is the Winter Hill mass trespass of 1896. Yes, we all know about Kinder Scout, but half a century before, 8,000 people stormed the gate that had been erected by one Colonel RH Ainsworth JP of Smithill's Hall to close off these longstanding paths and to protect his right to shoot defenceless grouse in the name of sport.

When the walkers got to the gate, they were met by the colonel, several heavies in his pay, and the police. Undaunted, the walkers jumped over the gate (eventually knocking it down) uprooting the 'Trespassers Will Be Prosecuted' notice and throwing it into the ditch with loud cheers.

The following Sunday 12,000 turned up to claim
and exercise their right to walk these rights of way. The
demonstrators were well aware that they ran the risk of
being prosecuted for trespassing, which would be very
serious for ordinary working people both financially
and because a criminal record would jeopardise their
employment opportunity. But they stood their ground.

I was up Coal Pit Road with a collection of walkers
who come here every year on Walt Whitman's birthday,
the American poet of equality and democracy who has
long-standing links with the town. They showed me the
stone with some pride, erected to commemorate the
centenary of the event (when 1,000 people turned up but
the atmosphere was much more cordial) and to mark the
opening up of most of the hill as access land. Now you
can wander here to your heart's content without fear of
anything nastier than the odd boggy patch.

Walking in the countryside is seen by some as a genteel
pursuit and, yes, it can be. We walk to escape the hurly-
burly of urban life, to get away from noise and rage and
clamour. But it's worth remembering that walking and
walkers also have a long and proud tradition of dissent and
protest. Modern 'rambling' began to a large extent as a
result of industrial workers seeking fresh air, recreation and
beauty after a week spent in the fetid heat and noise of the
mills and factories.

Disputes over access are not entirely a thing of the past.
I still encounter locked gates and barbed wire on rights
of way and you still hear of walkers being intimidated

and harassed. But things have got better, and that's in no small part due to folks like those who disregarded Colonel Ainsworth and his gate.

So if you're in these parts anytime soon, get yourself up Winter Hill via Coal Pit Road and feel a sense of pride and pleasure at walking in the footsteps of walkers past whose strength of conviction means we can enjoy our countryside in freedom.

The ice creams are pretty good too.

Walking the Wainwrights

2 14 Lake District hills and mountains bask in the glory of being a 'Wainwright' fell. Two decades after climbing his first Wainwright, author and broadcaster Stuart Maconie laced his boots to walk to the top of his 214th, 'the culmination of a love affair…'

It's a good question for us walkers at the best of times and it was especially appropriate now. Thick, clinging mist, 'clag' as it's poetically known, was hanging all around us. We were cold and wet and getting colder and wetter, unseasonal but typical Lake District rain pelting down from a sky as grey as the slate they mine at Honister, now lost in the murk far below us.

Normally, the answer to that question would have been 'No.' I'm not one of those macho, hairy, SAS fellwalker-types for whom the exertion and achievement is all. Walking for me is all about enjoyment. Usually I'll turn back happily if the weather or the clock or the blisters are against me. After all, the hills will always be there for another day, as Alfred Wainwright often said.

But it was him who got me into this in the first place. And now this was the last place, literally.

My last Wainwright mountain. Number 214. The final day of hundreds spent in this wonderful part of the world, often damp, often lost, sometimes scared, regularly exhausted but always thrilled to be here, metaphorically and physically above and beyond the cares and routines of the everyday world.

On any other day, maybe I would have turned back when the cloud and rain came down and we realised that we had drifted (or rather squelched) off Moses Trod path somewhere in the direction of Green Gable rather than towards Beck Head.

We were off-course for the summit of Kirk Fell, the only summit in the Lake District that was still terra incognito to me, the only one where I'd yet to get out the battered flask and the squashed buttie, throw down the pack, get out the Wainwright book and drink in that sense of literal and actual elevation that never paled or flagged.

So this wasn't any other day, this was a day that I'd planned and schemed for, and unless it became dangerous, turning back was not really an option. Looking around me, I could see good, slightly sodden friends who'd accompanied me on many a fellwalk in the past. Sodden, yes, downhearted, no. They wanted me to do this as much as I did. And in any case, there was champagne in the rucksack and an order placed for fish and chips 22 times at the Angel Lane Chippy in Penrith.

Beer and G&T were chilling in the fridge somewhere back down there below the cloudline at the gorgeous, sprawling pile in Blencow rented for just this occasion. So, until 'Do you always press on to the top regardless?' became 'Are you out of your mind or what?' we were carrying on. Moses Trod was somewhere over there, according to the GPS, and the rain was at least only relentless now rather than horizontal. If memory served, I'm sure it had sometimes rained en route to the previous

213 summits, although I could be wrong. We were going back a few years after all.

We were going back almost a couple of decades to be honest. The legendary fellrunner Joss Naylor completed a circuit of all the Wainwrights in just over a week, but mine had been a more leisurely, random and decidedly unmilitary approach. I hadn't even realised that I was 'doing the Wainwrights' until I was a dozen or so in, a couple of summers after that first day on Loughrigg Fell.

I bet Loughrigg is many folks' first Wainwright. It's handy for Grasmere and Ambleside and the fleshpots of the touristy Lakes. It's straightforward – just follow the crocodile of Gore-Tex – and it's not that tough, although the steady steep pull up the grassy flank has had friends of mine swearing on August afternoons.

But I can still vividly remember that first time.

I'd come to the Lakes often as a teenager, but when my wife asked me what those big hills were that were dominating the skyline I had to confess I didn't know. I knew the pubs and the curry houses and the lakes themselves, but when it came to what I now know is the real beauty of this part of England, its spectacular and varied landscape, I was clueless.

One pair of boots, a rucksack and a newly purchased blue *Central Fells* volume of Wainwright's *Pictorial Guides* later, we were headed for Loughrigg. When that little book came out of said rucksack a few hours later, when we stood and identified the distant peaks with help from Alfred Wainwright, when I realised that just a little effort

on foot could take you into a fabulous new world whose
dimensions and horizons couldn't even be imagined from
the speeding cars or the teashops below, I knew that this
was the beginning of a love affair. It wasn't an intellectual
decision, it was a physical churning of pleasure. I knew I
was going to do this again.

When I'd done it a few more times – learned to love
that feeling that AW calls the 'exhilaration of the summits',
the views, the sensations, the ritual of the flask and the
butties and the scanning of the skyline, Wainwright guide
in hand be it Silver How or Starling Dodd – a thought
occurred to me. Why not do them all? By nature, I'm not
a box-ticker or a completist. I've got records but I'm not a
record collector. I've never owned a stamp album. I don't
keep football programmes or crisp packets. But ticking
off the Wainwrights would mean that I would get to visit
every corner of this place I'd come to love; the pretty bits,
the remote bits, the hairy ascents and the hands-in-pockets
strolls. So I would do them all, all 214, at my own pace
and to suit my own schedules.

That's how it ended up taking so long. I grew to love
some bits so much that while I've still only been to the
top of Helvellyn once (or is it twice?), I used to go to the
summit of Sale Fell every Christmas Day. Getting a base in
the Ullswater area meant that I've been visiting Great Mell,
Souther and Bowscale Fells regularly, and neglecting old
friends in the south and west. I'd been stuck on 211 for a
couple of years, prompting much amusement from those
who've been following my (slow) progress.

What was needed was decisive action and a commitment that I couldn't wriggle out of. I decided that I'd get Steeple and Scoat Fell done as part of the Wainwright Society's 214 Challenge in the spring and then finish with Kirk Fell on June 20th, 2009 come hell or high water or, this being the Lake District, creaking knees and drizzle. Good advice for those trying to give up smoking is to tell all their friends that they are going to do so on a certain day, peer pressure and public scrutiny being an aid to the resolve. So, working on the same principle, I booked a castle, arranged a party and told all my walking friends that they were coming to the top of Kirk Fell with me on the Midsummer Eve, my final Wainwright.

Kirk Fell had remained elusive until the end thanks to its remote position in Wasdale and the lack of any quick, easy route up or down. I certainly wasn't doing it 'up the front', the ascent that Wainwright spends pages and a few comical illustrations decrying. After discussions with Eric Robson, David Powell-Thompson and John Burland of the Wainwright Society, I decided to approach it from Honister. It was the longest way but the most gradual and the easiest for the less-energetic of our party which was some 14-strong by the time we were pulling our boots on in a thin drizzle at the Slate Mine car park.

The question about 'pressing on regardless' came around about the time when the path disappeared from under our feet and the hills became cloaked in dense cloud some half-a-mile out from the ruined Drum House at the top of the pass. It was looking decidedly dicey. Rain ran from every jacket and cagoule, hands were getting too cold to hold maps, there were grazed shins and leaking boots. Spirits were high but I wondered whether I was in danger of letting my own personal quest get in the way of fun and common sense.

I was on the verge of calling it a day and trudging back to the castle for a welcome if undeserved champagne and chip supper when a couple of things happened. Firstly, thanks to some skilful GPS work, we found ourselves back on the grooved, ascending track of Moses Trod. I like a good path under my feet and if I know where I'm going, I can go a long way. So this was heartening.

Then a shape started to emerge through the murk. It was black and forbidding. Indeed it was the sheer rock wall of Gable's eastern face. But seeing it was a good sign; it meant the mist was lifting. Within minutes, the rain and cloud had gone and, with a flourish worthy of curtain-up on opening night, the glittering vista of Buttermere and Crummock Water opened up beyond Haystacks. To the left was the long wooded valley of Ennerdale. And somewhere up there was Kirk Fell.

There were still a few sticky moments to come, like jumping the stream on the way to Beck Head Tarn. And when it became clear at the tarn that, yes, we were going to have to go up that sheer rocky face, the one we could see people picking their way down nervously, then there were a few muttered oaths. But resolve never faltered for a second. In truth, I was touched. Everyone here could have been sipping a nice malt whisky in a cosy pub inglenook or playing Boggle in front of a roaring fire. But they wanted me to do this and they wanted to be with me.

Finally getting to the top made me soppier still.

It was a perfect moment, one I'll never forget; being in my favourite place with my favourite people. And more than that, it was the culmination of a love affair with these wild places, places that had taught me many things about what really matters in life and shown me things about myself that I would not have otherwise known. As I looked over Wasdale, over to Yewbarrow and Buckbarrow and shapely, distant Seatallan, across deep and enigmatic Wastwater to the shining Irish sea, over to the lonely sheet of water that is Burnmoor Tarn and, to the left, to the commanding heights of Scafell and Scafell Pike and Lingmell, I remembered long happy days on each one.

But no time to waste. There were pictures to take and corks to pop and, somewhere miles away and far below in Penrith, there was a smokey sausage with my name on it.

The Wainwrights

Here's the full list of all 214 Wainwrights, complete with their respective height in feet.

No	Hill	Height (ft)
1	Scafell Pike	3,208
2	Scafell	3,162
3	Helvellyn	3,118
4	Skiddaw	3,054
5	Great End	2,985
6	Bowfell	2,959
7	Great Gable	2,949
8	Pillar	2,926
9	Nethermost Pike	2,923
10	Catstycam	2,919
11	Esk Pike	2,903
12	Raise (Helvellyn)	2,896
13	Fairfield	2,864
14	Blencathra	2,847
15	Skiddaw Little Man	2,837
16	White Side	2,831
17	Crinkle Crags	2,818
18	Dollywaggon Pike	2,814
19	Great Dodd	2,811
20	Grasmoor	2,795

21	Stybarrow Dodd	2,765
22	Scoat Fell	2,759
23	St Sunday Crag	2,756
24	Eel Crag	2,752
25	High Street	2,716
26	Red Pike	2,709
27	Hart Crag	2,696
28	Steeple	2,686
29	High Stile	2,647
30	Coniston Old Man	2,634
31	High Raise (High Street)	2,631
32	Kirk Fell	2,631
33	Swirl How	2,631
34	Green Gable	2,627
35	Lingmell	2,624
36	Haycock	2,614
37	Brim Fell	2,611
38	Dove Crag	2,598
39	Rampsgill Head	2,598
40	Grisedale Pike	2,595
41	Watson's Dodd	2,588
42	Allen Crags	2,575
43	Thornthwaite Crag	2,572
44	Glaramara	2,568
45	Great Carrs	2,558
46	Kidsty Pike	2,560
47	Dow Crag	2,552
48	Harter Fell (Mardale)	2,552

No	Hill	Height (ft)
49	Red Screes	2,545
50	Sail	2,536
51	Wandope	2,532
52	Grey Friar	2,526
53	Hopegill Head	2,526
54	Great Rigg	2,513
55	Candale Moor	2,502
56	High Raise (Langdale)	2,499
57	Slight Side	2,499
58	Wetherlam	2,499
59	Mardale Ill Bell	2,496
60	Ill Bell	2,483
61	Hart Side	2,481
62	Red Pike (Buttermere)	2,477
63	Dale Head	2,470
64	Carl Side	2,447
65	High Crag	2,440
66	The Knott	2,423
67	Robinson	2,417
68	Harrison Stickle	2,414
69	Seat Sandal	2,415
70	Long Side	2,408
71	Kentmere Park	2,394
72	Sergeant Man	2,394
73	Hindscarth	2,385
74	Clough Head	2,381
75	Ullscarf	2,381
76	Thunacar Knott	2,372

77	Froswick	2,362
78	Birkhouse Moor	2,355
79	Brandreth	2,344
80	Lonscale Fell	2,344
81	Branstree	2,339
82	Knott	2,329
83	Pike O'Stickle	2,326
84	Whiteside	2319
85	Yoke	2,316
86	Pike O'Blisco	2,312
87	Bowscale Fell	2,303
88	Cold Pike	2,299
89	Pavey Ark	2,296
90	Gray Crag	2,293
91	Grey Knotts	2,287
92	Rest Dodd	2,283
93	Seatallan	2,270
94	Caw Fell	2,263
95	Great Calva	2,263
96	Ullock Pike	2,263
97	Bannerdale Crags	2,241
98	Loft Crag	2,230
99	Sheffield Pike	2,214
100	Bakestall	2,208
101	Scar Crags	2,204
102	Loadpot Hill	2,201
103	Wether Hill	2,198
104	Tarn Crag (Longsleddale)	2,178
105	Carrock Fell	2,165

No	Hill	Height (ft)
106	Whiteless Pike	2,165
107	High Pike (Caldbeck)	2,157
108	Place Fell	2,154
109	High Pike (Scandale)	2,152
110	Selside Pike	2,148
111	Middle Dodd	2,145
112	Harter Fell (Eskdale)	2,142
113	High Spy	2,142
114	Great Sca Fell	2,135
115	Rossett Pike	2,132
116	Fleetwith Pike	2,125
117	Base Brown	2,120
118	Grey Crag	2,093
119	Causey Pike	2,089
120	Little Hart Crag	2,089
121	Mungrisdale Common	2,077
122	Starling Dodd	2,076
123	Seathwaite Fell	2,073
124	Yewbarrow	2,060
125	Birks	2,040
126	Hartsop Dodd	2,027
127	Great Bourne	2,020
128	Heron Pike	2,007
129	Illgill Head	1,998
130	High Seat	1,994
131	Haystacks	1,958
132	Bleaberry Fell	1,935
133	Hipman Knotts	1,926

134	Brae Fell	1,922
135	Middle Fell	1,909
136	Ard Crags	1,906
137	Hartsop Above How	1,902
138	Maiden Moor	1,889
139	The Nab	1,889
140	Blake Fell	1,879
141	Sergeant's Crag	1,873
142	Outerside	1,863
143	Angletarn Pikes	1,860
144	Brock Crags	1,840
145	Knott Rigg	1,824
146	Steel Fell	1,814
147	Lord's Seat	1,811
148	Meal Fell	1,804
149	Tarn Crag (Easdale)	1,804
150	Hard Knott	1,801
151	Blea Rigg	1,774
152	Lank Rigg	1,774
153	Rosthwaite Fell (Bessyboot)	1,771
154	Calf Crag	1,761
155	Great Mell Fell	1,760
156	Whin Rigg	1,755
157	Arthur's Pike	1,745
158	Gavel Fell	1,725
159	Great Cockup	1,725
160	Whinlatter	1,722
161	Bonscale Pike	1,719
162	Crag Fell	1,715

No	Hill	Height (ft)
163	Souther Fell	1,712
164	Eagle Crag	1,706
165	High Hartsop Dodd	1,702
166	Sallows	1,691
167	High Tove	1,689
168	Mellbreak	1,679
169	Broom Fell	1,676
170	Beda Fell	1,669
171	Hen Comb	1,669
172	Low Pike	1,666
173	Little Mell Fell	1,657
174	Dodd	1,646
175	Stone Arthur	1,640
176	Green Crag	1,604
177	Grike	1,601
178	Wansfell	1,597
179	Longlands Fell	1,584
180	Sour Howes	1,584
181	Gowbarrow	1,579
182	Armboth	1,571
183	Burnbank Fell	1,558
184	Lingmoor Fell	1,538
185	Barf	1,536
186	Raven Crag	1,512
187	Grey Stones	1,496
188	Great Crag	1,496
189	Barrow	1,492
190	Cat Bells	1,479

191	Binsey	1,466
192	Glenridding Dodd	1,450
193	Nab Scar	1,443
194	Arnison Crag	1,420
195	Steel Knotts	1,417
196	Low Fell	1,387
197	Buckbarrow	1,377
198	Gibson Knott	1,377
199	Fellbarrow	1,364
200	Grange Fell	1,345
201	Helm Crag	1,328
202	Silver How	1,292
203	Hallin Fell	1,271
204	Walla Crag	1,243
205	Long Fell	1,223
206	Latrigg	1,207
207	Troutbeck Tongue	1,194
208	Sale Fell	1,177
209	Rannerdale Knotts	1,164
210	High Rigg	1,161
211	Loughrigg Fell	1,099
212	Black Fell	1,059
213	Holme Fell	1,040
214	Castle Crag	951

What is a Wainwright?

A Wainwright is a Lake District hill or mountain
that features in one of legendary guide writer Alfred
Wainwright's seven *Pictorial Guides to the Lakeland Fells*.
At first glance the figure of 214 fells seems arbitrary, and
Wainwright was reticent about how he drew up his list.
He based his selection firstly on height – all bar one of the
fells exceeds 1,000 feet, Castle Crag being the exception
at 951 feet. His second criterion was the hill's prominence
and whether it stood alone or whether it was merely the
shoulder or slope of another fell.

But location also played a part.

To make his task achievable, Wainwright effectively
drew a line around the extremities of the lakes to create
a reasonable circle, and then artificially extended the
northern boundary between Bassenthwaite and Ullswater
up to Caldbeck to include the fells north of Skiddaw.

His cartographer's ring did exclude a number of fells
that exceed 1,000 feet, about which Wainwright would
later write warmly in his *Outlying Fells of Lakeland* book.
Gummer's How, for example, on the south-east shore
of Windermere, tops out at 1,054 feet, and is 'a fellwalk
in miniature, a little beauty, with heather, a few rocks to
scramble on, soft couches for repose, a classic view and a
rustic Ordnance column.'

Planning the Wainwrights

Much of the excitement and satisfaction that walkers derive from ticking off the Wainwrights comes in the planning, long evenings spent hunched over maps, glass in hand, plotting the next walk, linking paths and summits to knock off a couple of fells in a single walk.

But if adrenalin starts to course in your veins and you want to accelerate your Wainwright-bagging without repetition, hesitation or deviation, then read Stuart Marshall's *Walking the Wainwrights*, where 36 circular walks cover all 214 peaks. Visit www.sigmapress.co.uk

For the seven wonderful *Pictorial Guides to the Lakeland Fells* by Alfred Wainwright, visit www.franceslincoln.co.uk

The Completers

The Wainwright Society maintains a list of walkers who have reached the top of each of the 214 Wainwrights. The complete list involves about 230,000 feet of ascent (the equivalent of about eight Mount Everests) and 710 miles of walking, yet the youngest completer was just 5 years old. Robin Regan finished the challenge in April 2009, having climbed Binsey aged just 2 years and 11 months in April 2006. For more information on everything Wainwright, visit www.wainwright.org.uk

Lethal
Combination

'When Cows Attack' sounds like a feeble parody in a not very funny TV sketch show. But if the notion was ever funny, it's become a lot less so recently. In 2009, Liz Crowsley, 49, and – in what is a bitter irony – a vet, was trampled by cows against a drystone wall on a stretch of the Pennine Way near Hawes. It was the latest in a series of attacks over the previous few years, several of which have ended in fatalities. Even when they haven't, the victims have often been badly injured and severely traumatised. In 2004, a woman in Derbyshire was stamped upon by angry cows in what sounds like a terrifying ordeal…

'Before I knew it one of the cows actually started charging towards me,' she said. 'The next thing I knew I was flat on my back, there was a great amount of bellowing and the many other cows joined in… I found myself in what felt like a scrum being butted and kicked… I was clutching my stomach and gasping – it felt as though it was going to split open.'

After that incident, Jim Turvey, farm manager at Brackenhurst Agricultural College in Nottinghamshire, commented on the rarity of such attacks, saying 'In general, cows are placid, gentle creatures. In 24 years I've never been hurt by one or felt threatened by one… but I have seen them go for dogs and it's a problem that is going to get worse with the right to roam.'

Hmm, that last bit has a whiff of expedient propagandising to me. And according to my anecdotal researches with country folk, these incidents are not that rare. It seems that, with or without their dogs, many farmers are injured each year by cows that have just calved, often happening when they try to comply with official regulations by putting ear tags on calves shortly after they are born.

The lethal combination here is 'dogs' and 'calves'. At the sight of a dog in the same field as her young, even the most docile bovine can become enraged and fiercely protective. If you can avoid taking your dog through a field of cattle, then do. And if you can't avoid it, the advice I've been given is to let the dog off the lead, especially if the cows look agitated. If the situation does turn nasty, dogs can move a lot quicker than cows; they'll skedaddle sharpish and the cows will usually be satisfied to see Fido off.

If you've not got a dog with you, all the usual rules apply. Give them a wide berth, walk quietly and quickly, don't get between a cow and her calf. Oh, and by the way, according to my rural sources, if you are faced with a field containing both cows and a bull, don't worry too much about the latter. He will be far more interested in the cows than you generally, unless you happen to be particularly cowlike and gorgeous.

You see, I've fallen into the trap there too. The notion of a cow attack seems so ridiculous that people don't take them seriously enough. When a former Home Secretary was trampled and injured on a birthday walk, headlines like 'Udderly Terrifying' and 'Birthday Boy Blunkett Bested by Bovine Bully' seemed somewhat callous, whatever you think of politicians. This was, after all, a blind man who was very nearly killed. The fact that David B himself made light of it in several interviews and newspaper pieces shows how we cowophobes feel embarrassed and silly about our misgivings.

Well, not any more. From now on, the nearest I'll try to get to Daisy will be indoors, specifically the dining rooms of pubs and restaurants. And no, I'm not joking.

Viva Stalyvegas!

Stalyvegas, the locals call it, though its proper name is Stalybridge, a town built on weaving and farming nestling in the high ground where the tidal sprawl of south Manchester breaks on the foothills of the Pennines.

A regular listener correspondent of mine lives hereabouts. She tells me that the Stalyvegas nickname comes, she thinks, from the fact that seen from the train or the road, the twinkling lights of the hill town evoke Nevada's tacky desert jewel. This is cute but most people think that the name also reflects Stalybridge's wild, mad, hedonistic, rough diamond feel. Just the place, then, for a country walk!

It's 15 minutes from Manchester Piccadilly and then out into a glorious late summer afternoon, armed with the instructions on one of a series of leaflets about Greater Manchester's abundant yet somehow secretive countryside. The general perception of this part of Lancashire is of dark satanic mills, cobbled streets and sulphurous factory chimneys. But nearly all of these mill towns are built in or near the countryside; rolling moors, open fields and small ranges of hills.

When I was a child growing in the urban sprawl of Wigan, a few hundred yards from my front door were the 'flashes'; great sheets of reedy water on the sites of former mine workings where huge carp, geese and swans could be found, and where the canal sluices were thick with a weed we called 'Nanny Green Teeth' which was reputed to pull you down into the depths of the murky water.

This was to me the boundaries of the known world, the border where the familiar streets and houses of my town gave way to a kind of wilderness. Since then I've always been fascinated by the idea of the 'Darkness on the Edge of Town' to quote a Bruce Springsteen album title; the places where civilisation peters out, loses its grip and a stranger, older order takes hold.

A few strides from the small Stalybridge suburb of Carrbrook village takes you on to the Pennine Bridleway where, gaining height, Manchester's skyscraper hotels and Jodrell Bank come into view across the town. But it's not long before all this is left behind, like the small farms and the weavers' cottages, and the air freshens and you're contouring round the hill and along Brushes Valley, where the first of four hidden, lonely reservoirs come into view.

Climbing on the reservoir road, I pass several men with those squat muscular dogs that seem compacted of anger. Their owners, despite shaved heads, are as friendly as their dogs seem fierce, offering route advice and cheery banter. When the service road gives out as if exhausted, open moorland is reached. The hills of Derbyshire are blue in the distance and now the scattered reminders of things man-made include a ruined cottage, a memorial to a dead gamekeeper and the constant throb and roar of the stacked jets waiting to land at Manchester airport.

The 20-minute crossing of the moor is the best part of the walk. This is Harridge Pike, a contraction of Hare Ridge, and in winter it's said you can see white hares up here. At one point, incongruously, the path becomes as sandy as the Ainsdale dunes before the Iron Age fort at Buckton is spied across the valley. Evidence of man far older than airports and reservoirs.

The merry, raucous jangle of ice cream vans down in the Tame Valley reminds me that it's the school holidays so there'll be no problems getting a cab back to Stalybridge: no school runs for the cabbies today. The buffet bar here is legendary: real ales, hot Vimto, black peas and quirky furnishings. I sit at a picnic table and look out at the town. The kebab shops and fun pubs of Stalyvegas will be lively tonight. But up above this little town, like all these little towns dotted across the north, is something much wilder.

Going Up the Wall

If the following is poorly spelled and littered with typos, then let me put in a feeble plea of mitigation. I'm not writing this at my normal computer. I'm tapping cautiously on one of the three keyboards in the back room of the Twice Brewed Inn in Northumberland. The polite but firm notice alongside my keyboard reads, 'Please note the computers are part of the vital village network for Northumberland. Please do not attempt to install anything on the computer.'

Frankly there's no chance of that. Even the simple act of typing is proving arduous right now. For one thing, it's 7am and I'm not really a morning person. For another, every muscle in my lower body is competing with its neighbour to find a new and exotic way to ache. And for yet another, the smell of grilling bacon from the breakfast room is tantalising beyond words. But the sun is shining for the first time in three days, the forecast is good and ahead lies perhaps the most exhilarating stretch of the Hadrian's Wall National Trail.

I'm doing it along with the team from the *Radcliffe and Maconie* evening radio show on Radio 2, broadcasting nightly as we go, a mad but fun idea hatched no doubt in a pub when we realised that we were all keen walkers, and that a long, outside broadcast visiting the parts of Britain often overlooked by the media was an interesting concept.

I can tell you now that it's not just interesting. It's been exhilarating, fascinating and downright exhausting. Since the first paragraph, by the way, I've e-mailed this to myself and am now, through a technological feat even Roman engineers would have found impressive, picking up the writing of it 13 miles and a day's march later on in a hotel room in Chollerford overlooking the North Tyne. So at this stage, with over half the trail and indeed half of England behind me, I feel qualified to give you a few personal thoughts and observations.

If you are planning to have a go at this new-ish National Trail then you, like us, may well have people telling you that you can do it in a weekend. And indeed you can, if your idea of fun is 25-mile days, blood blisters, sleep deprivation and knackered knees.

This is a trail to be savoured, particularly the middle section which switchbacks, big dippers and rollercoasts its way over Caw Gap, Steel Rigg and the Whin Sill Ridge. The landscape hereabouts is vast, empty and awe-inspiring and fans of the Lake District like me will find their hearts gladdened by the combinations of crag and lough.

Which brings me to another observation. 'They' will also tell you that the trail is flat. 'They' are either cruel pranksters or they have done the wrong trail. True, there is nothing here like the ascent of Scafell. But you'll feel your heart pump and hamstrings stretch on some of the ascents and descents.

Some of the toughest bits, either by virtue of squelchiness or gradient, have been pitched or paved. But this is an absolute last resort. This is not just a walkers playground, remember. It is one of the most significant historical artefacts on earth; the northernmost frontier of the world's most powerful and advanced empire ever. Here, walkers must share with and even defer to historians and archaeology. From Mithraic temples to abandoned Roman building sites to Bronze Age burial chambers, this walk is not just scenically stunning but full of the mysterious and fascinating echoes of our past.

Finally, if you are planning to walk Hadrian's Wall, come between May and October when the ground can take it and you can get your special passport stamped. And bring plenty of spare socks and waterproofs. And go easy on the draught White Hot and the Tarmonath Gold at the Twice Brewed Inn...

It's No Sweat Shop

The Countryside Alliances and Clarissa Dickson Wrights of this world are always keen as mustard to remind us townies that the countryside is a place of work and not just a lovely spot for light recreation or a playground. A little grudgingly, I take their point. But I know this too: that as workplaces go, it has a great deal to recommend it over, say, a Taiwanese sweat shop or Sheffield foundry. And that there is nothing wrong with playgrounds.

I thought about the notion of the countryside as a playground for very different classes of people on a weekend I spent in Derbyshire and Yorkshire. The Friday afternoon found me in the former county, and specifically in a lovely old-school hotel pretty much in the grounds of Chatsworth House.

Chatsworth is as handsome a building as England has to offer, the ancestral seat of the Dukes of Devonshire and, of course, the Duchesses. In fact, the house owes much of its current glory to the restoration efforts of the current Dowager Duchess, the former Deborah Mitford. Youngest and now only surviving member of the infamous Mitford Girls, she didn't get mixed up with Hitler, Oswald Mosley, get sent to prison or go off to fight in the Spanish Civil War. She devoted herself to her husband, Andrew Cavendish, and to the upkeep of Chatsworth, the 'Palace of the Peak'.

You have to say that she's done a grand job. And in return, she can enjoy perhaps the best back garden in

England. The estate is vast, there are farms galore on it, and the farm shop alone employs a hundred people. But for me the real glory is the open land. On the afternoon I was there, the trees were russet, the River Derwent serpentine and silvery and the adult stags were roaring just feet away from me, a sound oddly reminiscent of a malfunctioning outboard motor but you can see why it does the trick with those upstart bucks.

There is no getting around the fact that this is private land, with all the associated thorny issues and matters of historical contention. But it is stunning. And you have to admire the Devonshires for their policy of keeping fences and unfriendly signage to a minimum and letting visitors wander at will, an enlightened attitude that began with the 11th Duke and earned him praise from the ramblers. And me too, as I wandered back to my hotel along the banks of the Derwent in the last rays of what can only be described as a perfect autumn afternoon.

Ilkley Moor is a different sort of playground. An hour or two up the country from Chatsworth, this is where the millworkers, mechanics and miners of Leeds and Bradford have come on their rare days off for hundreds of years. Their pilgrimages here, on summer evenings and Sunday afternoons, have of course been immortalised in song.

Hatless, as the song decrees, we made our way up there on a bright October morning in which it was nevertheless possible 't'catch thi deeath o'cowd.' Fortunately, the flags were flying at White Wells, the famous bath-house turned café on Rombalds Moor, which meant that this quirkiest of teashops was open for Oxo, beans on toast, pie and peas.

The moor itself is vast, bleak and sombre, an entirely different kind of playground compared to the gentle loveliness of Chatsworth. You wouldn't want to get lost up here, not least since a supposed alien abduction in 1987. But it is wonderful, the kind of haunting, barren beauty that would drag you back again and again, and would linger in the mind when you were back at the loom or the coalface, and remembering how, for one day a week, you were free to play.

A Festive Chuckle

If you're familiar with the online streaming music services Last FM and Spotify (if not, ask a friendly nine-year-old – they'll be au fait with them), and you fancy a festive chuckle, find the Norm MacDonald sketch *Twelve Days of Christmas* from his *Ridiculous* album in which he gets increasingly exasperated with the various birds, groups of people and diverse flora and fauna that his true love is sending him. (When the lords start leaping, he concludes in desperation, 'I think we should start seeing other people!')

BE WARNED, THOUGH! This is about the most mainstream thing the acerbic, nihilistic Canadian has ever recorded. Don't listen or watch anything else by him unless you've got a tough hide for bracingly dark, sweary stuff. I haven't usually. But I make an exception for Norm. Anyway, it got me thinking about the Twelve Walks of Christmas, a variety of strolls, treks and rambles that will surely be familiar to many of you. You may have your own list but here are a few suggestions of mine, in roughly chronological order…

1 The urban ramble

Usually undertaken around December 22nd or maybe 'Mad' or 'Black Eye Friday', the traditional last day of work before the Christmas hols. It often involves gangs of young secretaries in Santa hats and fake reindeer antlers teetering in unsuitable footwear as they make their way from Pizza Express to All Bar One for another few Chardonnays. You wouldn't want to make your way up Jack's Rake in those heels, I can tell you.

2 The last-minute present

Normally a solo expedition undertaken by a harassed, red-faced man at four o' clock on Christmas Eve trying to get something for his wife. He has left it far too late and he knows it. The garage forecourt flowers or Boots gift token is often a prelude to divorce.

3 Homeward weave after pub crawl

Mountaineers rope themselves together for safety and security. Blokes put their arms around each other as they attempt the midnight return leg from various hostelries through darkened, icy streets. This makes progress difficult but does encourage shouts of 'I bloody love you,' 'You're my best mate' and 'I would give you my last pint and that's the truth.'

4 South face of Tesco

(Other supermarkets are available)
Christmas Eve is the traditional date for this tried and trusted excursion, most popular in holiday towns such as Keswick, Holyhead, St Austell and Hawes. It is particularly popular with nice families heading to self-catering cottages for the break. Mum can be seen putting salad, celery and fresh orange juice in the trolley whilst dad and kids add Pot Noodles, coke and 36 packs of salt and vinegar crisps. Just before the store closes, the family will return for the

stuffing and crackers they went in for originally but
have forgotten.

5 Walking the dog

A dog is for life of course, but if you have ignored 20 years
of public information films, you will have to exercise the
new arrival at some point. And of course any existing
canine family member is an ideal excuse for a proper
country walk. Or at least a brisk excursion to the park
or pub to get away from another epic Boggle session or
Top Gear DVD.

6 The fashion parade

Popular for many years now, the route of this favourite
can vary. What is essential is that at least one of the party
must be a teenage girl who is not only hugely resistant to
the idea of 'wandering about in fields freezing' but is not
going out 'looking like that' (indicates sensible older folk in
bobble hats, cagoules, etc). Consequently she sets out for
Cadair Idris looking like one of Girls Aloud in micro-skirt
and diamanté choker.

7 Christmas Day constitutional

For many years, mine was Sale or Ling Fell in north-west
Lakeland. These days it tends to be Dunmallard Hill or
Greystoke Forest over in the east. Be realistic about what
you can tackle. The day will be mainly taken up with
presents, eating, snoozing and phoning up distant friends.
And be prepared to wish every other walker you pass

'Merry Christmas' and have a little festive chinwag. It's dark at 4.30pm, remember.

8 *The hangover cobweb clearer*
Somewhere between Christmas and New Year you will 'accidentally' drink an entire gift bottle of Baileys/ schnapps/Jagermeister/Brazillian liqueur whilst watching a DVD box set of *The IT Crowd* or *Sherlock Holmes* or playing 'Super Mario Olympics' on the Wii or backgammon with your auntie. Consumed with self-loathing you will set out to climb a hill the next day to 'blow the cobwebs away' and almost pass out above Thirlmere. I know, believe me.

9 *Luring the kids away from the Xbox*
'Right, you've been sitting in front of that flipping thing for three days. Let's get a bit of fresh air and work up an appetite for that turkey jalfrezi we're having later. Now, no moaning. Boots on and… Oh, I didn't realise *Jason and the Argonauts* was on. Classic. Actually it does look like rain…'

10 *First day of the sales traverse*
Tackle the steep, crowded tourist routes up the stairs of Cotswolds and George Fisher on the day after Boxing Day clutching unsuitable anorak, stocking filler hat two sizes too small or elaborate hi-tech GPS device suitable for trip to Saturn but you can't work out where the batteries go.

11 New Year's resolution

Quick stroll down to sea, through park or up some minor elevation, prompts rash decision to walk coastline of Britain/every Corbett in Wales/all the Dolomites/ Katchenjunga before end of year. Will be quietly forgotten about around March.

12 Last one before back to work

Always a melancholy trip. The downside of the modern expandable Christmas season is that around January 3rd, sad, pallid figures who've existed on cheese footballs and sherry for two weeks can be seen on top of Whernside or along the Ridgeway looking moist-eyed into the winter sunset and thinking that in two days it'll just be a screensaver of this lovely view. But it will all be there waiting for you 365 days of the year.

Blue-Sky Thinking

It was with a producer friend of mine about a possible film script we were working on, a kind of walker's road movie set on the Hadrian's Wall trail. More on that as and when it ever blossoms. But I wanted to tell you about the meeting itself. There were no suits, no croissants, no bottles of Highland Spring, no flip-charts and no Blackberries. Well, actually maybe a few late-flowering ones in the ragged hedgerows alongside the muddy lanes and high moorland tracks in the High Peak above the Goyt Valley in Derbyshire. Because this was a walking meeting, one conducted on foot, on the move, on a brisk early winter's morning, one where the refreshments were carried in rucksacks and the agenda was set as much by weather and daylight as by 'any other business'. And it was an unqualified success.

My congenital dislike of meetings is one of the reasons I've made a very poor office worker on the few, forlorn episodes I've tried it. I'm either exasperatingly bossy and desperate to move things along, or equally exasperating in my lackadaisy (I think I've just invented this noun and I'm really rather pleased with it).

I once read in one of those dreadful blokey business manuals called *The Art of the Five Minute Desktop Warrior,* or some such, that no meeting should go on longer than an hour. Archie Norman, the supermarket svengali of Sainsbury, Asda, House of Commons and ITV fame, used to conduct his meetings in rooms with no chairs. Having to stand meant business was conducted briskly and, one would imagine, with a great deal of unnecessary stress

STUART MACONIE: NEVER MIND THE QUANTOCKS

heaped upon the already weary cubicle rats.

No thanks Archie. For anybody who's lucky enough – and I do realise it's a real luxury – I can recommend the alfresco meeting conducted as you tramp. The creative energies unleashed by walking have long been acknowledged by artists and musicians. Elgar would 'pom pom' his compositions to himself as he wandered his beloved Malvern hills. Modern composer Sir Peter Maxwell Davis gets his best ideas, he says, whilst walking the deserted beaches and dunes of his homes on Sanday and previously Hoy, both in the Orkneys. Indeed you can often hear the thin keening of sea winds in the reeds and marshes in his symphonies and string music.

Of course what I was up to was much more prosaic than Sir Pete. We were merely thrashing out some sticking points, getting new ideas, 'blue-sky thinking' if you like. But it was generated under a real blue sky, albeit flecked with storm clouds, not a strip-lit meeting room, and all the better for that. The simple fact of putting one foot in front of another, of climbing slopes, vaulting gates, crossing streams, seemed to liberate the imagination, unblock the thought processes from their cramped, constipated urban deadlock. We got more done in an hour on these quiet Derbyshire hills than we'd managed in a month of e-mails and a calendar of coffee shops.

The late, great poet Thom Gunn put it well in a poem called *On The Move*, a kind of existential hymn against inertia. Keep these lines in mind next time you come up against some brick wall, personal or professional. Trust me.

It works…

'At worse, one is in motion; and at best,/Reaching no absolute, in which to rest,/One is always nearer by not keeping still.'

Virtually Brilliant

The idea came to me while doing the 'Free Jogging' routine on the Wii Fit. Now don't laugh. I know there will be craggy, bearded solo-mountaineering types and sinewy, lycra-clad free jumpers and such who are, at the very mention of Nintendo's cutesy little fitness game thing, now snorting into their pint of Ruddocks Old Intransigent or steroid-enhanced protein shake. Well, pshaw! I like it.

But I think they're missing a trick. In the jogging mode, you trot around what seems to be a Bavarian market town. With a beach. And a massive waterfall in a cavern that looks like something out of *Avatar*. It's quite diverting. But as I jogged along, I began to wonder. Wouldn't this be more fun if the virtual scenery was High Cup Nick? Or Dartmoor or Pen Y Fan? The technology must exist, as my own primitive efforts in the medium confirm.

About ten years ago, I bought a tiny camcorder – well, it was tiny then, it seems as huge and unwieldy as a combine harvester compared to its modern equivalents – in order to film my fellwalks. The idea, and it seemed a reasonable one, was that when that sad day came when age, infirmity or some other undreamt of eventuality prevented me from actually getting my boots on and getting up there, these would both rekindle fond memories and act as a virtual walk. I could retrace my steps and get a sense from my armchair of at least some of what I'd felt when I'd actually been striding along the Hopegill Head ridge or clambering up Scarth Gap or having my butties at Alcock Tarn.

In truth, I've hardly ever looked at the resultant films, even though I've burned them on to DVDs for posterity. In fact the only ones I do seem to recall are those where something has gone markedly and entertainingly wrong. Like the 40-odd minutes of footage filmed inside a rucksack when a stray banana or some such released the pause button; a dark and abstract study in disorientation that makes Andy Warhol and Derek Jarman's most experimental work look like *Holiday on the Buses*. Or my record of a New Year's Day ascent of Bleaberry Fell, conducted with a raging, brutal hangover and complete with groans, unscheduled stops and erratic, dizzying camera work.

But just because my efforts were unsatisfactory doesn't mean convincing virtual walking can't be done. A quick googling session reveals that indeed there are several people doing it. One offers 'Virtual Walk DVDs filmed in beautiful and historic European locales for use while exercising on treadmills, ellipticals, exercise bikes, spinners, and Nordic tracks. Our Europe scenery DVDs actually will make the time you spend exercising fun!'

There's nothing like a jaunty exclamation mark to make me suspicious. But some of the above sounds appealing, especially the bit about treadmills.

The treadmill may be the most boring piece of machinery ever invented. It doesn't help that you usually find it in a gym, where the scenery is either a Lady Gaga video, *Sky Sports News* with the sound turned down or the other gym users, typically a man who keeps looking at himself in the mirror whilst he does one sit-up and then parades around huffing and puffing for 20 minutes. Wouldn't I go to the gym more often and with more enthusiasm if there were some way of convincing myself I were in Ennerdale or Sutherland or the Dolomites?

Of course no DVD could replicate the real thing. The leaking flasks, renegade sheep and the socks full of water. Or the nice stuff, like a pint outside a village pub or a sunbathe on a felltop. But I'm working on it. And I'm sure I could interest James Cameron in *Bleaberry Fell 2: The Hangover Continues.*

The Lion
and the Lamb

B reaking my own unwritten rule never to begin with a proverb, let us celebrate the month of March which 'Comes in like a lion and goes out like a lamb.' Weather proverbs are a branch of ancient lore that I find particularly opaque. 'Cast not a clout 'til May is out' for instance. I have never been really sure what that means, though I think it might be something to do with not taking off your long johns in a hurry, in the unlikely event that you were wearing them in the first place.

Then there's 'April borrows three days of March and they are ill.' Pardon? And that one about rain on St Swithin's Day only really works if you know when St Swithin's Day is. If I've ever known, frankly it's gone. Sorry Swithin. (Ed: July 15th!)

But that old saw about March's leonine entry and lamblike departure does seem to have a ring of truth about it. And this year I am ready for a soft cuddly lamb of a spring. Normally, I love winter. I love short days on the snowy hills, sparkling vistas, what Tennyson beautifully described as 'the long glories of the winter moon,' and crunching my way back to hot baths and drams by the fire. But in the words of one George Harrison, the winter of 2009/2010 felt like a very 'long, cold, lonely winter.' And, yes, 'It feels like years since it's been clear.'

So, here comes the sun? Well, not necessarily. But I think I speak for a lot of people when I say that I am ready to welcome spring with open arms. The darkness and sleet and chapped hands and travel chaos of winter has seemed enervating rather than bracing. Maybe it just came on too hard or went on too long. But I'm certainly ready for a bit of gambolling.

Clearly, spring gets people like this. On the CD shelves in front of me, I have Noah and the Whale's *The First Days of Spring* album and Talk Talk's *The Colour of Spring*, both dreamy, swoonsome, vaguely sensual affairs. Casting my eye into the classical section (I really must get around to alphabeticising this one day) I spy Aaron Copland's *Appalachian Spring*, Stravinsky's *Rite of Spring* and Debussy's *Printemps*. All very different but all imbued with feelings of renewal, vigour and life bursting out of its winter prison.

So where to go for a spring walk? I've been leafing (Ha, leaf! Spring!... Oh, please yourself) through a ramblers' booklet containing 20 suggestions for spring walks. Some are new to me and sound enticing, like the Beacon in the Chilterns or The Norber Erratics (who I think I once heard in session for John Peel) in a newly opened area of the Yorkshire Dales National Park.

I have to say that the inclusion of the Stiperstones in Shropshire surprises me a little. I love the Stiperstones but it's a grim, forbidding parade of stones more suited, I'd have thought, to horror films, old *Sherlock Holmes* movies and bleak mid-winter days.

No, for a spring walk you want somewhere you can see those first green shoots, hear a bit of birdsong and enjoy that extra hour or two of daylight. The Malverns perhaps, or the Cotswolds. Somewhere where the roaring lion bits of March won't be too rough and the lamby bits will be positively delightful.

So, yes, bring it on. I've had enough of snowmen and sledging for another year. And when the frosty season rolls around again, I shall of course employ another piece of venerable weather lore to aid in my predictions...

Onion skins very thin
Mild winter coming in;
Onion skins thick and tough
Coming winter cold and rough

So, if you see me doing some furtive feelings in the fruit and veg aisle at Tesco, you'll know why.

War of the
Roses II

J ust off Junction 37 of the M6 lies the town of Sedbergh. Nice place it is too. Literature fans will enjoy its 'book town' status. There's a good and diverse music festival every June. And the walking's good. The town nestles at the foot of the Howgill Fells, Wainwright's sleeping elephants, and you can wander here all day, from Winder to Arant Haw, from Cautley Spout to The Calf, and sometimes not see a soul, even on a Bank Holiday Monday.

On the main street there's a shop that for years boasted my favourite sign in all the world, one that I mention often during my book talks about Middle England and that has even been immortalised as one of my radio jingles. In thick black marker on a hand-made poster in the shop window it reads 'Please note; we do not sell lightbulbs or batteries!!'; the 'not' and the 'or' treble-underlined for emphasis.

This speaks volumes about some of our national traits. Because clearly the only need for such a sign is if a fairly constant stream of people are entering the shop asking sheepishly for the aforesaid items. In the USA, land of Victor Kyam, Bill Gates and Henry Ford, I'm pretty sure they'd be getting a box of both put by. Not here. There's something hilariously, vexatingly English, something very 'folded arms' and 'we've never done that sort of thing here and we aren't about to start' about it.

Sedbergh, or rather the countryside hereabouts, has been at the heart of a very English row. Or a very Yorkshire one anyway. Essentially discussions have been afoot on boundary changes to extend the Yorkshire Dales National

Park further into parts of Cumbria and Lancashire. Already Sedbergh is in this curious position of being in the county of Cumbria but the Yorkshire Dales National Park. However under recent proposals, the Northern Howgill Fells, Mallerstang and Wild Boar Fell, Middleton, Barbon and Leck Fells, Firbank Fell and the Lower Lune Valley would all be included in the National Park. And in the event of this extension of course, it starts to become problematic that park be known as the 'Yorkshire Dales'.

Yes, there's a whiff of Anschluss and an echo of the Sudetenland – a very, very gentle echo of it – around this gorgeous, lonely part of England. And, unsurprisingly I'd say, but then I'm Lancastrian, most of the fuss is generated east of the Pennines. You see, it's being mooted that the National Park be renamed the Dales and some folks are reet brassed off abaht it. There is, inevitably, a Facebook campaign. I just looked at it on the site and saw almost immediately, and just as inevitably, the phrase 'God's Own Country'.

A member of the Yorkshire Dales National Park Authority, Mr Blackie, said: 'There must be some geographic anchor if we are to keep the Yorkshire Dales special. The scenery is iconic and is the very definition of what Yorkshire is about.'

'If we do not protect the name and identity, then we are doing the people of Yorkshire a great disservice,' Poul Christensen, chair of Natural England said when announcing the start of the consultation.

I can sort of see their point. But I can also see that the

good folk of the disputed bits of Lancashire will not take kindly to being absorbed into anything bearing the name Yorkshire. We do have a bit of form in this regard. Look up the Battle of Towton if you don't believe me.

Does it matter? Will Randygill and Yarlside be any less lovely? Will Nine Standards Rigg become any more humdrum? Will Wild Baugh Fell become any less austere and wonderful? Will they start to sell lightbulbs and batteries in Sedbergh? I'll keep you informed.

Terpsichorean
Muse

J ust as John Cleese' increasingly irascible customer in Monty Python's 'Cheese Shop' sketch puts it, 'I delight in all manifestations of the Terpsichorean muse,' it was the fact that walking in the country cleared my head of music that helped me come to love it. Perhaps that's not entirely true. Perhaps it was the clamour of the music business more than the songs and pieces themselves that I was happy to leave behind. But certainly when I became a walker in my mid-20s, part of the attraction of lonely moors, high fells, lakes, forests and wild places in general was that it was a world apart from the sticky carpets, plastic glasses of fizzy lager, laminated passes, baggage carousels, hotel lobbies and tour buses that filled my 'working' hours as a rock journalist.

It wouldn't have occurred to me then to take music into the countryside. Wasn't there music enough there already? That's what the purists would say anyway, usually going on to mention the delicate trilling arpeggios of birdsong or tinkle of waterfalls. I sort of agreed with them. I was pretty keen to leave the jangle of the indie guitar bands behind and cleanse the aural palate with an outdoor sorbet. Besides, the iPod was still just a gleam in Jonathan Ive's eye.

But even the purists would have to acknowledge that British composers down the years had drawn inspiration from the landscape and tried to reflect it in music. Elgar and Malvern is the obvious and celebrated relationship here, all that rich Edwardian melodicism just perfect for those lovely, gentle and homely hills.

Vaughan Williams is thought of – wrongly – as a pastoral composer when really he loved cities and hated his music being characterised as 'cowpat music'. But his 'The Lark Ascending' is perhaps the most famous and best-loved evocation of nature and the English landscape. Like pretty much everyone else with ears and a heart, I adore it; usually finding myself swallowing hard around the middle section. But he also wrote 'A Norfolk Rhapsody' and a tone poem called 'In the Fen Country', both of which have the bleaker and more muted charms of those particular quiet corners of England.

I always associate William's beautiful 'Phantasy Quintet' – as lovely as 'The Lark Ascending' but much less well-known – with a lambent sunset on the grassy, rounded slopes of Whinrigg and Illgill Head, the gentle back view of the Lake District's Wastwater Screes. The reason being that I heard the quintet for the first time on a battered Walkman as I took an after-dinner stroll from a cottage by Devoke Water one summer's evening. But I also connect that view with the exultant psychedelic guitars of the first Stone Roses album, the new favourite my mates had blasting from the kitchen CD player when I returned.

Pop music can work as landscape soundtrack every bit as well as the more obvious accompaniment of classical music, just as long as it's the right sort. These musical musings have been prompted by the fact that on my regular four-miler over the tops by Greystoke Forest en route to my (sort of) local, I thought I'd let the MP3 player choose a few tunes at random to accompany me. I would never have picked the ones the clever little gadget did, but the selection was sensational and serendipitous. I can now tell you, though you might not have guessed it, that the work of early 70s experimental electronic John Peel faves Tangerine Dream is just perfect for the spooky depths of a silent forest, and that particular albums by American gloom rockers The National and quirky folk harpist Joanna Newsom are quite ideal for austere Pennine views and frolicking lambs respectively.

Silence is golden, and yes, the natural sounds of the outdoors are unimprovable. But I could enjoy a new career that I feel beckoning; bespoke walking soundtrack consultant. Unusual and thought provoking pop tunes for your favourite walks. Nick Drake and Clifford T Ward for the Clent Hills, Fleet Foxes for Kielder Water, Joy Division for Stanage Edge, that sort of thing. And guaranteed, no Simply Red, Spandau Ballet or Chas 'n' Dave. Some prejudices die hard I'm afraid.

Dig Deep
for MRTs

For sale, one Land Rover. Twenty-seven years old and with only 14,000 miles on the clock. Sounds like a bargain, eh? But wait 'til you hear about those miles. Suspension-sapping off-road crunches up boulder-strewn bridleways, stiff climbs up the Walna Scar road in snow drifts and sheet ice, slides down scree runs, fording fast-flowing rivers.

I am one of those intolerant folk who see red at the sight of a 4x4 on the streets of a town or city. But this is one that has never done the school run or the Ikea bank holiday jaunt. This is a vehicle that has lived. And forget about 'one careful owner'. This has had about 30, and I wouldn't call them careless exactly. But they have sometimes forgotten the niceties of 'mirror, signal, manoeuvre' when they've been putting the pedal down and crunching through the gears as they head up to Goats Water in their quest to find a fallen climber.

That Land Rover is coming to the end of its working life as part of the fleet of three used by Coniston Mountain Rescue Team. So, anyone who can spare a new one or the cash needed, get in touch. You might be thankful of it yourself if you ever put a foot wrong on Dow Crag or twist an ankle on Wetherlam.

Even though they're not my local team, I'm the patron of Coniston MRT, partly because, well, they asked me, and partly because I'm Lancastrian and before the mid-70s boundary changes and creation of Cumbria, Coniston and its fells were part of Lancashire. I'm not really sure what patrons are supposed to do beyond put their name at the top of the letter-headed notepaper. But maybe it's things like this; telling you a bit about Mountain Rescue Teams and encouraging you to support them.

I met Jeff and Rob at their base at the top of the village, where the platform of the old station used to be before Dr Beeching wielded his axe and did his best to ruin the nation's public transport system. As a cheeseparer par excellence, Beeching would have approved of the Mountain Rescue since they provide a valuable public service without costing the government a red cent.

As I'm sure you know, MRTs are all made up of volunteers and they are funded solely from voluntary contributions. This might be your handful of shrapnel placed in a tin on a village shop counter or pub bar. Or it might be a donation from a grateful rescuee.

'Sometimes, a walker that you pick up in difficulties will give you a few quid or whatever they've got on them,' they tell me. 'They're often pretty frightened and disoriented. And then a month or two later, you often get a more substantial cheque and it turns out in the meantime they've organised some kind of fund-raiser to say thank you.'

Like most MRTs, Coniston's men (and women) prefer to remain voluntary funded as it gives them a certain flexibility and independence from state control (although they'd like more cash for sure). But they're keen to stress that not all MRTs feel the same and there are cordial differences of opinion. Outside of the well-known and much-frequented tourist destinations such as the Lakes and

Peaks and Snowdonia, some teams struggle to survive on donations. Jeff's firm – all MRTs have regular jobs as well as their rescue work – stump up for equipment and I learnt from an issue of *Mountain Rescue* magazine that Goodyear paid for a new tranche of laptops for MRTs.

From the same publication, I also learnt that there exists an organisation called Amputees in Action who supply limbless actors 'who can simulate major clinical traumatic injuries for any incident, regardless of scale.' Beneath a picture of a grimacing one-armed man dripping with (hopefully) fake gore, was their slogan 'We lose it, you use it.'

Marvelling at the ways of the world, I take my leave of Jeff and Rob. I'm down the road at a rented weekend cottage for a friend's birthday celebration and it's my turn to cook and chill a few jugs of sangria on this May evening, the nicest of the year so far.

Walking down the hill into the village, I reflect that whist I'm sitting round the table eating, drinking and having fun, Jeff, Rob and their team mates may well have their sunny Sunday shattered by an emergency call and an evening expedition into the high crags for a night of sweat and struggle and searching for some lost soul who could be you or me. So next time you see that tin, dig deep...

Personal Bests

Alfred Wainwright's reputation as the original grumpy old man is, shall we say, not entirely undeserved. In his wonderful books, he was always likely, apropos of little or nothing, to moan about the number of people who took the tourist route up the Old Man of Coniston, or football hooligans, or to expound confidently and wrongly that 'all fellwalking accidents are the result of carelessness' (which must be scant consolation if you've just been blown off Sharp Edge in a Force 8 gale).

He later cemented his irascible image in the public's imagination by a series of monosyllabic TV appearances in which he'd appear in a voluminous anorak, smoking a pipe and scowling through teashop windows at the clag on Skiddaw saying things like 'this is in for't day,' like Harold Wilson in a particularly gloomy Ingmar Bergman movie.

But in the terrific conclusion to his *Pictorial Guides* in the last few pages of *Book Seven*, a different Wainwright emerges. Tender, elegiac, enthusiastic and capable of a phrase that always brings a lump to the throat: 'The fleeting hour of life of those who love the hills is quickly spent, but the hills are eternal. Always there will be the lonely ridge, the dancing beck, the eternal forest, always there will be the exhilaration of the summits.'

These concluding pages also contain his summing up of his 'personal bests' from Lakeland, a chance for the old grouch to enthuse a little, in a manner that pre-dates the enthusiasm for lists and trivia by at least a decade. Allow me my two-penn'orth in belated but topical response.

The finest half-dozen fells, then. I'm with him on Gable, Blencathra and Pillar. They're not just big; though they are, satisfyingly so. They're shapely too, with the latter demanding to be climbed when you see their distinctive summits from afar. But Scafell Pike? Yes, there's the sense of achievement that comes from knowing you stand higher than anyone else in England (apart from a few hundred cabin crew). But does anyone feel much affection for the relentless, stony ascent and the bleak, overcrowded lunar landscape at the top?

Then there is his list of 'best places for a fellwalker to be', topped off by the now 'no-go area' that is Lord's Rake on Scafell. Most of these are disappointingly hairy and blokey. It seems he didn't rate a place unless sheer drops and vertigo were on the agenda. Having dangled in the jaws of Mickledore myself (another of his faves) I reckon there are far better places for a fellwalker to be. Like Bowscale Tarn. Or the lovely top of Glenridding Dodd. Or the top of the Wast Water Screes. Or, for that matter, the cheese counter at Booths' supermarket in Keswick or several beer gardens of my acquaintance.

His favourite summits, though, are less macho and chosen judiciously with a connoisseur's eye for shape and elegance. Helm Crag is grand and Dow Crag a mountain eyrie that makes the ordinary walker feel like a Bonington or Hilary. Let me add one of my own: Steel Knotts, in the quiet and secret valley of Martindale. The actual summit is called, splendidly, Pikeawassa, and is a rugged rock outcrop that is perfect as a backrest on a summer's afternoon.

The ridge walks pick themselves, but again, is the steady plod of the Fairfield Horseshoe really better than the excellent couple of miles from Ullock Pike to Carl Side on Skiddaw? And as someone who agrees entirely with his ecstatic assessment of the dreamy, inviting, undulating traverse from Hopegill Head to Whiteside – he calls it the finest half-mile in the Lakes in another chapter – you can only wonder why he excluded this from that final list.

Ah, well. Maybe he was just in an odd mood that day.

Sea Fever

A thousand school anthologies have got it wrong. It's one of literature's most famous and widely disseminated misprints, right up there with 'all that glitters is not gold' (Shakespeare put 'glisters') and Coleridge's Ancient Mariner who actually said, 'Water, water everywhere, nor any drop to drink.'

So John Masefield, Poet Laureate from 1930 to 1967, really intended, 'I must down to the seas again, to the lonely seas and the sky' as the resonant opening line of his most famous work *Sea Fever*. But a succession of well-meaning but slovenly editors wrongly corrected it to 'I must go down to the sea again,' which ostensibly makes more sense but not when you realise Masefield was writing about seafaring rather than strolling.

The mistake makes more sense for me, though. I've never spliced a mainbrace or knowingly tied a clove-hitch but every now and then I must go down to the sea again, for my fix of lonely sea and sky, and some 'flung spray' and 'blown spume… and the wind like a whetted knife.'

And if the sky's azure blue and high pressure's cracking the barometer glass, I don't mind that either. In the last couple of years I have fallen completely under the spell of sea-walking and coastal paths. Having spent years in the hills and loving every second of that too, I'm delighted to have found a new kind of walking pleasure, one that can be just as energetic as hillwalking but carries with it different sensations and a different dimension of joy.

I write these words at a high balcony perch several 100 feet above Carbis Bay, Cornwall.

To my right, with some callisthenic craning, I can glimpse the long, low headland of St Ives and its higgledy-piggledy collection of houses and studios clustered like barnacles along its harbour. Its steep streets are crammed with surfers, shoppers, amateur artists and screaming stuka divisions of seagulls who'll have the 99 out of your hand in a trice if you're not vigilant. You can understand why the streets are crowded. The pasties and fudge are to die for, the Heligan Honey and Trelawneys Pride are a fine drop and there are more surf shops than you can shake a board at. But leave the crowds behind, take the winding road out along the bay and you see a different Cornwall and, for me, the real reason to come here. The sea – the real one, the lonely one – and the sky.

Yesterday I walked the couple of miles from the dramatic spur of Gurnard Head to the huge, graceful whale bulk of Zennor's headland. I met a handful of people, largely German interestingly, drawn perhaps to what we as an island race may have come to take for granted, the spectacular rock architecture of our coast and the endlessly changing theatre of wave and light and weather.

Round every twisting corner of path, there's something new to 'oooh' and 'ahh' at; a delicious secret beach without a single windbreak, a shadowy, sinister smugglers' cove battered by breakers, a fearsome finger of basalt pointing skyward from the churning sea. Above all it is the sea that draws you.

At heart, the difference between this and fellwalking is philosophical rather than physical. The exertion, the climbing, the striding out, the strolling is the same. What is different is the boundaries and limits. No matter how big the hill, at some point you will reach the top. The ground will be beneath you, the summit attained. When you walk along the coast, though, you are constantly reminded that you can only go so far, that there is another mysterious, shifting, churning, shape-changing domain that is forbidden to the ordinary walking mortal.

It is deadly. And lovely. That is why sailors tales are full of sirens and mermaids. That is why LS Lowry may be known for Salford's smoky backstreets but his deepest works are his vast, empty seascapes. That is why Isaac Newton used this wonderful metaphor for his life's work: 'I seem to have been only like a boy playing on the seashore, and diverting myself in now and then finding a smoother pebble or a prettier shell than ordinary, whilst the great ocean of truth lay all undiscovered before me.'

The sea makes awestruck children of us all, even the greatest of geniuses.

I have a few more days here yet. And there are irresistible names on my map – Hell's Mouth, Pendeen Watch, Three Stone Oar and Semphire Island. Sorry John, I know what you meant. But I must go down to the sea again, 'to the vagrant gypsy life... and quiet sleep and a sweet dream when the long trick's over.'

New Horizons

As I write these words, I'm gazing in awe at mountains. A fabulous ridge in fact, a curving dorsal razor-back of misty, jagged peaks that looks just about do-able without being one of those nutcases with the chalk and the carabiners, gently descending to the shores of a blue-green bay. It looks terrifically inviting. And I'll probably never get up there at this rate.

You may have guessed that it's not a British mountain range I'm looking at. No, it's the *Piccole Dolomiti*, the Little Dolomites, seen from a balcony in Verona where I'm having a weekend break. And looking at those gorgeous, only slightly distant mountains, has got me thinking about country walking and how, for me, that pretty much always means this country.

That's not an ideological decision, though, and let me be clear about this. I'm no Little Englander I hope, much as I love the misty isle of Albion. Venice and Austin, Texas, would be near the top of my list of favourite cities. Riding the Vaporetto on the Grand Canal or eating breakfast burritos on Sixth Street is my idea of heaven. But these are urban pleasures. It's the towns and architecture and lifestyles of these cities I love. As far as I can recall, if we don't count mooching about at the foot of the Eiger during a Stone Roses NME photoshoot and a two-day trek to the bottom of the Grand Canyon, all of my leisure walking has been done in Britain.

I wonder why?

Laziness is one reason. I like to be able to get out and about quickly. I spend a lot of time in Manchester and Birmingham, and I love the fact that within half-an-hour by car or train, I can be in Clent, the Malverns or the Peak District, boots on and striding out.

Even when I'm at my place in north-east Cumbria, I have to gird loins and make the effort to cross to the beautiful Western Fells. Souther and Blencathra, Carrock and Clough Head are much nearer and the more alluring for all that. Not least because I am also a lousy planner. If I pick somewhere close to home, at least it won't be far to turn back when I realise that I've forgotten my map/boots/butties or can't remember whether I turned the oven off.

Also I do love the British landscape and have yet to even scratch its surface. Its variety is becoming more apparent the older I get and the more I explore, from the almost Mediterranean glories of Cornwall to the rolling shires of the Cotswolds and Worcestershire, to the austere beauty of the northern moors and hills.

New Zealand's mountains look amazing, but can I bear a day and a fitful night in a sweaty, pressurised tube eating pretzels with my knees under my chin to get to them, especially when even Scotland's remoter beauties are only a few hours away?

I am told by people who know such things that Corsica is like the Lake District but with the climate of the Med. Sounds gorgeous, but then I do a bit of research and, learning that Corsica's public transport is negligible and its most beautiful village is accessible only by boat, Bowscale

Tarn and the Wyre Forest look deliciously close at hand for that early evening summer stroll.

But begone such parochialism! That glimpse of the *Piccole Dolomiti* has whetted my appetite and ignited my wanderlust. Recommendations gratefully received for foreign climes that I can get to relatively easily – a nearby airport would be useful – that would be comparable to the landscapes and treks I know and love at home. My horizons need expanding and I promise to bring you back some duty-free...

Will I Need
a Bow Tie?

Two Gore-Tex waterproof jackets, one smock-style, one zip-up. Seven pairs of walking socks, mainly merino but one waterproof (effective but slightly weird). Similar number of casual socks. Several T-shirts, mostly special walking wickable type, one bearing the legend 'The Phenomenal Handclap Band' and one saying 'Oldham, Home of the Tubigrip Bandage'. One Fred Perry shirt. Six 'smart' shirts for evening wear. Two pairs of 'all-day' trousers, two pairs of walking trousers, one pair of shorts, given the forecast, possibly optimistic…

I like the idea of long-distance linear walks. I like the sense of achievement. I like looking back over the map and seeing the ground covered, the path snaking inexorably towards its destination. I just don't like the packing. Most of my walks are done in a day, in an afternoon even, and so my idea of packing for a walk is a daysack containing: 1) a flask; 2) a map; 3) a pork pie. And even then I will forget the flask and end up having to stick my head at an awkward angle under a beck or pray the route takes in a 'rinky-dink' teashop.

So it would be fair to say that I'm a little stressed right now as I'm packing for my second major long-distance trek. Once again, it's for a series of outside broadcasts for my Radio 2 evening show, stopping off for fun and frolics and live music along Dorset's Jurassic Coast. Previously, we walked Hadrian's Wall from west to east (the sensible way, with the wind at our backs, whatever anyone says) and I managed the walk fine. The packing was an ordeal, though.

Several nights found me washing my walking trousers in my hotel sink and I had to buy some swimming shorts in a sports shop in Carlisle, having forgotten that one of the hotels had a pool.

Fabric boots or leather? Poles or no poles? The smallest decisions become magnified to Gordian knots of complexity at times like this. When I'm wild camping I can only take what I can carry on my back. Such strictures act as what philosophers call an Occam's Razor, shearing away all unnecessary palaver. Toothpaste yes, shaving foam no. You don't need to shave for a day but you will want to brush your teeth. And so on. But when you have the limited luxury and freedom of the van driven by our Sherpa Banjo Alan (he's called Alan and he plays the banjo – I wish it were a more interesting explanation too) then you can get the complications that come with choice. Should I take a spare pair of boots? Is there room for some extra contact lens solution?

Of course one person's essential is another person's effete luxury. In his guide to packing for long-distance walks, travel writer Mark Moxon acknowledges that 'it's a personal choice and everyone takes something different.' He doesn't take a deodorant for instance but he does take a sewing kit. Unless the nights are very slow I don't intend doing much in the way of embroidery. But I sincerely hope that my colleagues will be following my lead and packing the deodorant. Even thinking about the toiletries is beginning to bring out a film of perspiration on my forehead. Aftershave? You may think not? But what if I get asked out to dinner by the lady Mayoress of Lyme Regis? But then go too far along that route and you start to think you need a bow tie, possibly even a cummerbund.

But now I hear the distinctive rasp of Banjo Alan's van, if not his banjo, and Lulworth Cove beckons. I'll let you know what I forgot...

Wish You
Were Beer

'Water, water everywhere, nor any drop to drink.' As aforementioned, that's actually what Coleridge wrote in the *Rime of the Ancient Mariner*, though it is usually mangled into 'and not a drop.'

Anyway, what Sam and his mariners were bemoaning was the fact that you can't drink salt water. By reading 'Sea Fever' you will know that I've fallen completely under the spell of the coast. And in 'Will I Need a Bow Tie?', I was packing for a 90-mile trek along the spectacular Jurassic Coast of Dorset and Devon with my Radio 2 show. It was a joy, but Sam was right; you can't drink that briny stuff. And so, segueing neatly like some sort of DJ, let me tell you about some of the hostelries we sojourned in during the latter.

We made our way over high cliffs and crashing seas, down from Studland to Swanage and on to Weymouth. I'd imagined a seaside town of Georgian gentility. 'Maybe 200 years ago,' a local chortled in response. And yes, Weymouth of a weekend is a lively, somewhat cheesy place and no mistaking.

We struggled with hostelries initially, though. Banjo Alan, our trusty Sherpa, loved the biker pubs and got up to play harmonica with a somewhat startled acoustic balladeer in the Golden Lion.

But even he, a man who eschews real ale in favour of fizzy lager and John Smith's Smoothflow, found it hard to find a nice drop in Weymouth. A barmaid in one pub didn't know what a single-malt whisky was (for the long-distance walker it is the sleeping draught of choice). It looked bad for a while.

But then we found a harbour bar with actual sawdust on the floor and a pint whose name I've forgotten but which we liked enough to drink them dry of. Then a flurry of 'tweets' from helpful locals pointed us to The Boot ('behind the ugly council building') and we drank rough local cider until it was time to make our way back and pack the rucksacks for the 'morrow.

It got better after that. We rewarded ourselves for the steep ascent of Golden Cap (the highest point on the south coast and a reminder to sniffy northerners that it's not all bowling greens and rolling downs here) with a night in the aptly-named Beer, a gorgeous village on a secret cove where we filled the back room of the bar with music (from local legends Show of Hands) and people and empties.

The sun came out to meet us as we strolled the shingle of Budleigh Salterton and Sidmouth. Squeeze played 'Pulling Mussels From A Shell' in honour of our shellfish tea in the parlour bar of the Bedford Hotel. Delighted locals thronged the pavement looking in through the windows when the pub could hold no more. Then the victorious ladies' darts team arrived from an away fixture and the rest is confusion…

Don't believe them when they tell you it's all downhill after the pull out of Sidmouth up to Ladram Bay, where the Picket Rocks keep silent vigil. There are still enough switchbacks to test the calves and work up a thirst.

Reaching the high, lonely headland of Orcombe Point, where the Geoneedle marks the end of the Jurassic Coast Path, was a bittersweet experience. And the bitter was indeed sweet in the Royal Beacon Hotel that night, as Fisherman's Friends sang sea shanties and Edwyn Collins' guitarist Andy experimented with absinthe and Baileys.

Now I know what some of you are going to say. In these health-conscious days, responsible drinking is to be encouraged. And you are right. There was many a lime and soda and warming cuppa drunk too. But whatever your tipple, a good pub is a delight to a walker; particularly on the coast when the sea-mists come in and the spray soaks you through and the fishing crews (and the ladies' darts team) come home with their spoils.

No Direction Home

'How does it feel,' asked Bob Dylan 'to be out on your own, with no direction home?' Well, we've all been there Bob, haven't we? And it's good to know that even one of the most revolutionary and pre-eminent pop song writers of this or any other generation has sometimes found his navigational and route-finding skills wanting. But here I want to talk to you about a feeling that is even more dispiriting and deflating than finding yourself sans direction, and that's getting lost and bewildered whilst in full possession of a guidebook or, worse, a detailed route description.

Dufton Pike it was. I've liked the look of it for a few years now, a shapely cone standing sharply in relief against the backdrop of the higher Pennine ridge when viewed from the M6 or the eastern Lakes. Alluring in that way pikes are – like the mountain every child draws – even if there's more elevated company around. The sense of apartness I guess. Anyway, I had a free day and it didn't look any more like snow than it has every day since the previous October. And I remembered that my colleague had been up there in summer just before he'd joined me on my last Wainwright. His route had been detailed in the pages that I clutched in my hand as I strode confidently up the muddied track out of the village towards the hills.

I think it must be me. It has to be. Everyone has trouble with flatpack bookshelves. Everyone struggles with the new DVD player. But I seem to be one of the few people who have trouble with directions, even when they're limpidly

clear. Don't get me wrong. Don't think me a total fool.
I can read maps and I know my way around a GPS system.
The problem comes when human choices, tastes and
descriptions intrude on the cold factual world of contours
or co-ordinates.

On Dufton Pike, I was convinced I'd gone the wrong
way because there was no mention of the old ruined farm
I passed a mile out of the village. Convinced I'd gone too
far, I bore right too soon, slogged up the slope and then
slogged back down again, when I saw the unmistakeable
groove of the path that I'd quit too early winding invitingly
away a couple of 100 feet below me. Of course I now saw
that, as you'd think, the directions were bang on. It was me
of little faith (in myself) that was the problem.

It didn't really matter. The top of a pike is a pretty
unerring route-finder. The reason I'd gone wrong is that
I'm quite fascinated by ruined farms and they register with
me. So do funny looking trees. So do funny looking dogs
but even I know that they're not permanent fixtures of the
landscape. More sensible folk pay attention to conventional
guidebook markers – stiles, walls, gates, big signs saying
'Helvellyn This Way!!'

Another problem is that I've had to learn an alien
language, that of natural and geographical features. I grew
up in an environment where the most striking elements
of the landscapes were cooling towers, pylons and blocks
of flats. So when I first fell in love with the Lake District,
when first I wandered lonely as a newly liberated factory
chimney cloud guided by Wainwright, I was confronted by

an array of baffling new terms. What exactly was an arête? How about a declivity? How exactly was I to 'follow the line of the escarpment' when I thought an escarpment was a sort of breaded chicken thing? Of course now I am expert in all these things and I can lead you off a moraine-strewn arête avoiding the escarpment and down the declivity like a good 'un. But I still don't know if you count this thing here as a stile. I'd say its more of a gatepost. Hmm, maybe if we retrace our steps to that ruined farm…

A World Gone By

At the risk of destroying his widely held (and entirely deserved) reputation as a crabby old buzzard, my radio colleague Mark Radcliffe recently bought me a present. It is a rather beautiful small book called *The Rambler's Countryside Companion*, a facsimile of a slender 1950s Ward Lock guide called *The Wayfarer's Book* and written by one E Mansell.

I don't know if E Mansell is the fellow represented on the cover; a noble looking chap, with pipe, walking stick, shorts and woollen socks, but he looks a chap you could trust in a tight corner. Perhaps he is indeed harbouring fantasies of getting the young lady sitting beside him into a tight corner; a dreamy lass in a pale blue bonnet gazing over an impossibly beautiful, impossibly English dale. Cotton wool clouds drift across a serene azure sky and below them a silvery ribbon of river wends lazily to the hazy horizon.

Just inside this tempting cover, Mr Mansell explains the book's genesis: 'Some years ago, I was asked by a member of a rambling club to which I belonged, what was the meaning of the word lychgate. Not being able to give an explanation, I took the first opportunity of looking into the matter. From that day I have made it a duty and pleasure to keep a log of everything unusual discovered during my many wanderings. This little book is the result.' With this, Mr M is off, expounding and discussing, with I like to think, an airy wave of his pipe, 'barns, bench marks, bridges, churches, dew ponds, dovecots, haymaking, hopping, horse brasses, love spoons, market crosses, scarecrows, stiles, sundials, thatching, village greens, watermills, weathercocks, whipping posts and windmills.'

I'm a sucker for book nostalgia. Show me the green and white livery of a 1930s Penguin crime edition, or the stylised colour cover illustration of a Dean & Sons abridged classic (and what an abridger Mr Dean or his son must have been – my childhood copy of doorstop-sized epic of American literature *Moby Dick* was as thin as the *Highway Code*) and I'm in heaven. Give me a pulp sci-fi bug-eyed monster cover or a Ladybird classic or, yes, an original Wainwright and I'm straight off into a reverie, albeit a slightly mildewy reverie with some foxing on the frontispiece.

Savvy publishers, such as the ones behind Mr Mansell's charming guide, have realised the lure of retro-chic book design in the last few years. Witness the striking and alluring covers of, say, Marina Lewcyka's *A Short History of Tractors in Ukranian* by the brilliant Jonathan Gray, whose beautiful, nostalgic cover for my own *Pies and Prejudice* was, I'm sure, part of its appeal.

The photographs on the covers of some of the newer editions of Alfred Wainwrights's *Pictorial Guides* display nothing of the quiet, bygone beauty and precision of those pen and ink drawings.

Mr Mansell's guide doesn't just look deliciously antique. Its pages evoke a Britain gone by. The opening of the chapter on Shepherds and Sheep is typical: 'A good shepherd is generally the most independent of the farmer's

servants, jealous of his skill and reticent to a degree.'
I'm not sure I get that bit about jealousy. Or servants. A
shepherd of the author's acquaintance is described as 'a
grand weather-beaten old man of seventy-two summers,'
which is again a sharp indicator of how times have
changed. I doubt whether many 72-year-olds would call
themselves grand old men these days, not with Ringo and
The Stones coming up on the rails and with a suntanned
fellow of 82 summers being the star of BBC 1's Saturday
evening schedules.

Is this really a world gone by, though? Or one that never
really existed? Are such guides a real insight into the past,
or a gauzy, dreamy abstraction painted by Romantics of
a later era, evoking that same nostalgic shiver as Vaughan
Williams' 'Tallis Fantasia', of Elgar and Hardy. Or LP
Hartley's wonderful evocation of a lost, pre-Great War idyll
in *The Go-Between* which begins, brilliantly… 'The past is a
foreign country. They do things differently there.'

We certainly like to think so, which is why we love to
be guided through that foreign country by the likes of the
mysterious Mr M.

It's All in the Planning

I have about 40 favourite lines from *Gregory's Girl*, that wonderful film about teenage love in a Glasgow new town, but one of my very, very favourites is the moment when Gregory's little sister Maddie is given a huge and elaborate ice cream float in a café. Gregory looks on at the impressive and delicious sight and says 'Wow' or words to that effect. Maddie replies thoughtfully, 'The nicest bit is just before you taste it.'

This has always seemed to me a wonderfully perceptive remark about many a thing in life, but it certainly strikes a chord where adventures in the great outdoors are concerned. Getting out the maps, planning routes and itineraries, packing the gear, investigating refreshment opportunities; all of these have their own pleasures, separate from but sometimes almost as rewarding as the thrill of being out and about itself.

No one took more pleasure in planning an excursion than Lake District guide writer Alfred Wainwright. I knew this already of course from the many references to sketching and poring over maps by his Kendal fireside. But further proof came in the shape of a fantastic document kindly sent to me by Paul Holden in Blackburn.

Paul's late father-in-law Lawrence Wolstenholme was a friend and correspondent of AW. In fact it was to Lawrence that AW sent the famous postcard from Dent admitting defeat and abandoning (for an hour or so at least) his Pennine Journey, now a long-distance walk. As young men, they dreamed of organising a walking tour of the Alps, but

it remained just a dream because of cost and the demands
of exams and marriage. However, in 1939 AW drew up a
detailed itinerary for a 16-day excursion across the Bernese
Oberland. Once again, though, it remained just a fireside
fantasy; 1939, as Paul puts it, 'was not a good time for a
continental adventure.'

I have in front of me, though, that initial itinerary,
what is in effect Wainwright's first walking guide though
one that was never made public. It is a wonderful thing.
The 'prospectus' itself is perfectly feasible – 'Day One:
Blackburn to London, evening in London. Day Two:
London to Paris. Day Three: Paris to Neuchatel. Day Four:
to Gstadt by way of Fribourg and Chateau d'Oex…' and
so on to the glaciers of Grindlewald, the Blumlisalp Hut,
the Faulhorn, Interlaken and such.

But what makes this such a lovely artefact is the sense
of the mischievous, roguish, fun-loving young man that
comes through, so different from the perceived image
of the archetypal grumpy old man. There are cartoons
including one of the expedition itself (Wainwright in a
rakish fedora is styled Leader and Deputy Leader with
Wolstenholme as Porter), a page of the 'Last Words of
Famous Climbers' ('Watch me jump this crevasse,' 'This
rope's frayed a bit') and a section on the imagined joys of
the trip to come, 'an exhilarating descent, a sunset seen
over snow, a hot meal, an idle evening beneath a starry sky,
a hidden orchestra in the grounds of a nearby hotel, beer
gardens, beer…'

It is obviously a bit of fun for the amusement of workmates. But what shines through is a genuine excitement at the thought of making such a trip and meticulous and deeply felt pleasure in the job of planning itself. In the crude maps and the lyrical prose descriptions of the Alpine landscape, one can detect the seeds and stirrings of what was to become a style known to millions.

And tucked away in a flippant description of himself on the title page 'Our Leader Alfred "True Blue" Wainwright, Artist, Lecturer, Founder and Sole Member of the Wainwright Fellowship,' is one very significant sentence. 'Author Of *Wainwright's Guide to the Lakeland Fells*.'

AW never got to Switzerland. He never even went abroad. But some of the dreams in this young man's fantasy were going to come true. I wonder if he knew.

RIP Muffin

Some of you will know, in a manner of speaking, my little former walking companion, Muffin the West Highland terrier. There's a line about her ('he's happiest when fellwalking with his dog Muffin') in the blurb about me that tends to get reproduced on the jacket of my books. That's something I'll have to change because Muff is no longer with us, or at least not in furry body.

Muffin went to chase grey squirrels in the sky just before Christmas but she leaves lots of fond memories of great days on the hills and in woods and dale. She must have had a good hundred or so Wainwrights under her belt (or collar) and though she never ticked a list or opened a map she knew the Lake District hills well, even if she was generally more interested in any sheep to be spotted or the pork pie she knew was lurking in my rucksack, than views or geology.

She got us out of a scrape on Green Gable, though, when my wife and I became separated in thick mist and she ran to and fro between us as we called until we were reunited. She was the sole witness to a ring being given on Knott and to a near 'domestic' on Bakestall occasioned by high winds, steep scree and a badly tightened cap on a Thermos of coffee.

She observed all these incidents with the same air of slightly detached ennui, only showing any real enthusiasm when the rucksack went down and the aforementioned pork pie made its appearance. But she commanded attention with her Garbo-esque cool and on more than one occasion was the star of the day's adventures. Once, when she grew tired on the descent from Dodd, I popped her into the rucksack and she peeped over my shoulder for most of the return. Guys, forget what they say about taking a baby to the supermarket. If you want to have every woman in a mile radius rushing over to 'coo' and swoon over you, put a cute Westie in your backpack.

Muffin came with me several times to the Northern Fells and we once spent a damp, misty afternoon together wandering in circles on Bowscale Fell. So we decided that her final resting place should be Bowscale Tarn. We packed her ashes in the rucksack and went with her up to the hills one last time, up the rutted farm track made comically slippery by glassy ice and packed snow on a freezing Boxing Day.

When we got to the tarn, it was a grey sheet of ice a foot thick. We stamped our feet and blew on our hands and looked around for a good spot. Eventually we found the perfect one, just up the craggy fellside and off the beaten track but accessible enough for us to return to in all weathers. We said our goodbyes, scattered the ashes under a cluster of rocks and sat and looked down on the frozen waters and Christmas card scene.

It was a lovely moment. Sweet and tender and not remotely sombre or mawkish. Which is why I wanted to share it with you. Many of you will have made or be thinking of making such a journey, with a much-loved companion, animal or human. And if you're wondering what it will feel like, well, I can only speak for myself but it felt like a celebration and a tribute.

I'm not a fool or overly sentimental (I love the description of sentimentality as 'the indulgence of feelings you don't really have') but a sense remains that Muff's spirit is somehow up there in the lonely hills whilst her earthly remains lie at rest on the wild hillside. She feels at peace to me, resting after a short and happy life and I love knowing that, as the years go by, I can take myself up there and visit her, can sit alongside her for a while just as I did when she was alive, and share with her these wonderful places.

And though I'd be happier sharing it, there is something to be said for having all the pork pie to myself...

Rambling for
Progress

Broadcaster Clare Balding's text to me said it all really: 'Enjoy the best job on the radio.' She was right as ever. As I write, I'm three shows into my stint on *Ramblings*, the Radio 4 walking strand, covering for Clare for a series whilst she's occupied elsewhere. Hers are elegantly capacious boots to fill, she is frankly brilliant at whatever she does, whether it be sparring on *Have I Got News For You* or covering the Grand National.

Ramblings, a lovely programme that I'm sure many of you know, used to air on Sunday afternoons until someone realised that was precisely when many of its potential audience – walkers – would be out and about. Now you can hear it at what I'd call the crack of dawn (6.07am) on a Saturday morning or on Thursday afternoons.

I may tell you more about the show itself later. But for now I wanted to share with you the feeling I got from the first show we recorded. The idea of this series is walks for short winter days that are easily done from major population centres to give fine skyline panoramas of neighbouring cityscapes.

Late January took me to Belfast and a trip into the hills that provide the wild backdrop to that warm, tough, sometimes troubled city. I walked over Divis and the Black Mountain with a group drawn from the Glenn Walkers of West Belfast and the Ulster Federation of Ramblers. A hint of the care and tact and equanimity – and yes, sometimes silliness – that must still be exercised in Northern Ireland can be seen in the fact that Divis means the Black

Mountain, but both are used side by side. All traditions must be represented, even in the naming of hills.

All sections of the community were represented on our walk, too. It didn't take a genius to work out from the various home patches and forenames of my companions who belonged to which community. But the moment our boots were on and height was gained, the stuff of the streets was forgotten. This was a lesson in how putting one foot in front of another nearly always means progress.

Up on the Divis' windblown, domed summit, you could be in the wilds of Donegal, if it weren't for the ugly antennae of the ex-military listening post on the southern flank. It's a testament to how much progress has been made in the province, though, that many of the walkers told me how once this would have been forbidden territory to both sides of the community, bandit country in parts, army ground in others. Now you can climb all the way to the top and see Lough Neagh's vast sheet of blue, the largest proper inland lake in Europe.

And on the other side, you can see Belfast. You can see the ugly peace walls. But what you cannot tell from up here is who is who, and what is what. Nationalist and Loyalist streets look just the same from up here, tight terraces and dense estates filled with working-class folk just trying to get on with life. Billy pointed his phone's video camera at Cormac: 'Say something in Irish for the people of the Shankill, Cormac.'

'Something in Irish for the people of the Shankill,' joked Cormac, before delivering a lilting stream of Gaelic. It was a lovely moment, a jokey exchange that acknowledged difference but did not let it get in the way of friendship on the hills. Billy brings troubled young people up here from both sides of the political and religious divide. He told me that when they see how small their streets are from on high, and the evidence – cairns and mounds and furrows – of the original Belfast folk who lived in these hills millennia ago, it makes them see sectarian squabbles in a different way.

On the way down after a grand day I looked at some old fragments of pottery found in the hills and displayed in the visitor centre. Some bore the Protestant Red Hand of Ulster, others the Shamrock of the Republicans. 'Both made by the same pottery makers,' said Cormac with a wink, 'Religion's all well and good, but Belfast folk are very canny when there's money to be made...'

Walking, Talking Robot

If you have recently seen me striding purposefully by with an air of glazed and intense concentration and in the manner of a small child pretending to be a robot, you may have been tempted to shake your head sadly and reflect, 'I knew no good could come of listening to all those Belgian techno records.' But no. Years of aural outrage have nothing to do with this current vogue. You can tell by the way I use my walk I'm a Nordic type, no time to talk, as the Bee Gees so nearly sang. Well, actually we have a little time. So let me explain…

I first heard about Nordic walking from Billy Bragg, or rather in connection with Bill. When a mutual friend heard that I'd be walking some of the Jurassic Coast Path with Bill (the trail passes his Dorset doorstep) she remarked, 'He's not going to get you doing that Nordic stuff is he? He's into that.'

'That' turned out to be Nordic walking, a particular style of exercise using trekking-style poles developed in Scandinavia in the 1930s. Its original name 'Ski-walking' reflects its origins as an all-season fitness regime for cross-country skiers. There are those who will at this point scoff and suggest that walking is simply a matter of putting one foot in front of another and 'watching where you are putting your feet,' as Wainwright has it. But in order to get the proven health benefits of Nordic walking – a 90 per cent all-body workout with a 46 per cent increase in energy consumption compared to normal walking – you have to get the technique right. So I figured I'd do it properly and ask Tracy.

Tracy – who may well be reading this in which case 'Hello' – is a qualified Nordic walking instructor. Looking for something memorable to do for her 30th birthday, rather than other popular options such as drinking her own bodyweight in Bacardi Breezers – she Nordic-walked 30km a day for 30 days for charity. I had nothing quite so dramatic in mind. Even so I wanted to get it right which is how I ended up striding around Birmingham's Cannon Hill Park on a Saturday afternoon looking, well, like a small child pretending to be a robot.

The first thing to say is that whilst you can Nordic walk pretty much anywhere – rubber tips for pavements, spikes for countryside; Tracy regularly bounds up the Malverns this way – I found it a very different experience from my normal country walks. It's more focused and concentrated, especially if you're a novice like me and thus working hard on remembering the right gait and movement. I also found myself wanting to bound off briskly like a dog straining at a leash. There's something about the walking style that propels you along, which is great for fitness but less for chatting. In fact, I reckon that if you can chew the fat whilst you're Nordic walking, you're probably not going to lose much of the stuff you're chewing.

I loved it, though. It feels bracing and energising and I could certainly feel the pull in my shoulders and laterals. One downside, I guess, is the conspicuousness of the whole enterprise which means that, though you can do it anywhere, I'll be more likely to Nordic walk on a quiet country lane than, say, Piccadilly Gardens, Manchester. But at the end of my five miles round the tranquil Castle Sowerby roads in the Northern Lakes, I felt nicely sweaty and breathless. And no one asked me where my skis were. But I feel they will.

Liquid
Refreshment

A walk without water is half a walk for me. I don't mean the bottled stuff from Malvern and Ashbourne. That's nice to have but at a push Vimto, Theakstons or the stuff that comes gushing gratis down the beckside will do. No, I mean water in situ, in the landscape, whether standing in tarn or lake, flowing in ghyll or river or utterly untamed and unknowable as in the sea, the best of all.

It's good to know that other, frankly smarter folks than me, have had the same strangely primal feelings about bodies of water too. Wordsworth, fittingly for our pre-eminent Lake Poet said, 'A lake carries you into recesses of feeling otherwise impenetrable…' whilst his American counterpart Henry David Thoreau – who liked a particular stretch of water called Walden Pond so much that he chucked everything up and went to live next to it on his own – said that, 'A lake is the landscape's most beautiful and expressive feature. It is earth's eye; looking into which the beholder measures the depth of his own nature.'

Nearer our own time, even that arch grump Philip Larkin recognised the almost mystical nature of this pure and inchoate element. In a poem called *Water* in his collection *The Whitsun Weddings*, he wrote:

If I were called in
To construct a religion
I should make use of water.

Going to church
Would entail a fording
To dry, different clothes;

My liturgy would employ
Images of sousing
A furious devout drench,

And I should raise in the east
A glass of water
Where any-angled light
Would congregate endlessly.

Tarns have such a magical and enrapturing effect on me I sometimes worry, after I've dragged someone a 1,000 or so feet up to see one, that my companion will simply say, 'Very nice. Can we go to the pub now?' So it was gratifying that when I took my friend Deb up to Bowscale Fell – the easy, gradual if dull-ish way from Mungrisdale – she literally gasped when we came to the lip of the ridge and the shy blue teardrop was revealed hundreds of dizzying feet below.

Bowscale Tarn is a place I go back to again and again. 'Back in the day', as Adele and Tinie Tempah would say, it was a favourite spot on the Lake District daytripper's itinerary. Victorian ladies in crinolines and bonnets and their gentlemen friends in mutton chop whiskers and stovepipe hats – there is the faint possibility that I am resorting to stereotype here – would pick their way up the stony track from the hamlet to sit by the glassy waters cradled in the steep-sided shelf of the fellside and hope to catch a glimpse of the two immortal fish who were said to live in its inky depths.

But there are far too many loved and favoured sheets of water to list here quickly; bleak and lonely haunts like Floutern Tarn and Devoke Water, the high, imperious reservoirs of the Pennines, the Peaks and the Brecon Beacons, the jeweled pools of Clent and Shropshire. When I go to visit my mum and dad in unlovely urban Wigan, I even take a half-hour detour to the 'flashes' of Worsley Mesnes and Poolstock, quiet stretches of water set in a ravaged former mining landscape that marked the edge of the known world when I was a kid; a frontier fringed with mystery and adventure.

Yes, Phil and Bill and Henry were right. There is something special and other about these places, sacred even, these mystical places 'where any angled light would congregate endlessly.'

Win and Lose? Der!

It's a great place to shake off a hangover; a compellingly perfect cone rising between the long curve of Upper Edale and the gentle bustle of cafés and kit shops of Castleton.

It catches the wind from every direction, making it blustery and bracing and a fine vantage point for most of the Dark Peak, along Rushup Edge and the prominence of Mam Tor a couple of miles away via an enticing, undulating ridge over to the sombre high skyline of Back Tor in the north-east.

This is Lose Hill, a fine little climb from the hotel named after it, nestling down below by the Edale road and my base for this trip, just up a country lane from the village of Hope.

The night before had been a lot of fun, just like this short, invigorating pull, but very different.

I'd been talking with poet Simon Armitage and music critic Paul Morley about the current pop music climate at a Sheffield University literary festival event. It had been a fascinating and diverting hour or so. Then afterwards, a stroll though the genial mayhem of this lively city on a Saturday night, a drink or three at the bar owned by Arctic Monkey Matt Helders, and then a fuzzy-headed breakfast to the jingle of Morris dancers' bells in Leopold Square.

And then, the best bit, towards Glossop and the Snake Pass before swinging left across the causeway over Ladybower Reservoir and a date with the plucky little top with the plucky loser's name.

Lose Hill stands across a lush valley of mixed woodland, brimming with May blossom like foam breaking on shingle, from its twin peak Win Hill. On my first trip I didn't get the significance of the names; amazingly lots of people don't. And it is also known as Ward's Piece. But Win and Lose? Der!

The story goes that in AD 626, there was a great battle here between the armies of Northumbria and the combined might of Wessex and Mercia. Though the latter, under Cwichelm and Cynegils of Wessex, and possibly King Penda of Mercia, had the greater numerical strength, the Northumbrians proved more cunning and rolled boulders down on their advancing attackers from behind a defensive wall. The hill where the Northumbrians stood became known as Win Hill; its counterpart Lose Hill.

It's a nice story, and unlike many like it, seems to have some basis in truth. I'm glad because I do like a name with a story, or a hint of mystery, or even sometimes the baldest and bluntest of derivations.

A section of Lose Hill is also known as Ward's Piece. This is because in 1945 the local access campaigner GHB Ward was given a piece of the hill by the Sheffield Ramblers. I love the literalness of this. Ward's Piece was, yes, Ward's piece of the hill.

Up on the gusty summit of Lose Hill, there's a toposcope where the lover of evocative nomenclature like me can stand a while in the buffeting wind and relish the names on the skyline all around. Northerners will know just who one's Mam is, and yes, Mam Tor is literally

Mother's Heights, or possibly Breast Hill, but both names reflect its maternal, even matriarchal relationship with the valley below. But I like its nickname too: the Shivering Mountain, a reference to its notorious friability and instability and its frequent landslides and rock falls.

Look again at the toposcope. There's Ringing Roger, which sounds like a child's playground name or even something workaday to be done in the offices of Sheffield. And here's Grindlow Knoll, where surely grumbling dwarves have their council meetings. The names themselves would lure you even if the vista didn't.

Had I known what a scrappy non-event the FA Cup Final was to prove – I had to be back in my hotel room with feet up by 3pm as a matter of ritual – I'd have stayed up there longer; pressed on over that inviting switchback that struggles eventually up the flank of mum's hill, with its comforting shape, shivering next to Ringing Roger and the assembled dwarves of Grindlow Knoll.

Bad Steps and Puddings

We take as our text for today the words of Thin Lizzy, Joan Jett and Avril Lavigne who have all both warned of – and celebrated – the 'bad reputation'. Not hills and walks admittedly, but just as there are some people whose reputation goes before them, so there are tracts of countryside and expeditions whose dullness, toughness or general unattractiveness is the cause of ramblers' gossip and curtain-twitching. These are the walks that are 'no better than they ought to be' and just as with folks, often the tittle-tattle is unfair.

Take Mungrisdale Common in the Lake District, for example. It is perhaps the most maligned hill in England, routinely dismissed as a 'pudding', a 'lump' or even worse. And it's true that, if not for Wainwright's bizarre and perverse decision to include it in his volume on the Northern Fells (thus ensuring its place on the tick-list of all Wainwright baggers) few would bother exploring this rather unprepossessing height round the Back o' Skiddaw. But come over from Skiddaw House (rather than the pathless, pointless wander up from Mosedale) and this is a definite and distinct summit with interesting – okay, mildly interesting – rocky knolls and a cute if flat summit. For filmic evidence of this, see my DVD, *Wainwright's Northern Fells*, by the way.

Certain walks deserve their reputation for fearsomeness. Sharp and Striding Edges, Crib Goch, Jack's Rake, Sgurr Mhic Choinnich on the Black Cuillin Ridge. Words and phrases like 'exposure', 'sheer', 'rough', 'steep' and 'airlifted off by helicopter' tend to crop up again and again in the guidebook descriptions and, yes, the accident reports. Words like these make some turn the page with a shudder, whilst they are alluring and irresistible to others. In fact, it's the growth of the guidebook industry that has probably done the most to spread the reputations of these feared or hated mountains.

Back when only a handful of beardy types talked of secret routes in the back bars of remote pubs – a state of affairs I'm sure some of those macho cairn-destroyer-types still wish was the case – tales of 'bad steps' and the like would have been passed on in hushed tones to a handful of listeners. With the coming of the mass publication of guidebooks, individuals' personal preferences and foibles become enshrined in lore. Alfred Wainwright's feelings about 'puddings' and such become oft-quoted dismissals, as did Decca Records' famous rejection of The Beatles on the grounds that 'groups with guitars are on the way out.' Oops.

Mostly, though, bad reputations are gained not for being dangerous or scary. That, after all, has a certain sexy cachet. The real bad press is gained for being boring, a trudge, or worse a squelch, such as the vast moorland dome of Ben Chonzie in Perthshire, the mire of Bleaklow in the Pennines, the slog up Pen yr Ole Wen from Ogwen Cottage or the horrible shaley descent of Rossett Gill ('it gets better,' says Wainwright, lying).

So, let me say once and for all that Armboth Fell, the second most maligned Wainwright fell surely, is nothing like as bad as folks make out. Yes, you should choose your day, after a sustained dry spell or when cold weather makes the ground hard. But even when it's wet, there is nothing to fear but a soggy sock – the terrain at the Glastonbury festival is far, far worse I can assure you – and you will be rewarded by a cracking little rocky top and a sense of real and dramatic isolation on one of the Lakes' loneliest and most spacious ridges.

Keeping your eyes and ears open is a crucial skill for those of us who like to head out into wild places. But don't believe everything you hear about hills. Or even people for that matter.

The Great Leveller

By the time you read this, the lovely Clare Balding will have prised the 'best job on the radio', namely the *Ramblings* programme on Radio 4, out of my cold, dead fingers and it will be in her grasp once more. Okay, I admit that perhaps is putting it rather over dramatically. But it was such a joy to be out and about in all weathers – well, actually, just one kind of weather; bloody freezing – making these programmes with producers Maggie and Helen and a collection of lovely people from groups such as the lively Welsh Women Walking to probation officers in Lancaster, policemen in Bath, youth workers in Belfast and the poet Simon Armitage in the lonely Pennine Moors. Each day was different, each day was treasurable in its own way and every one will linger in the memory.

Just from looking at the projected programme list, I expected to learn things from my stint on *Ramblings*. Was the story about Garth Hill outside Cardiff true, that it was the actual hill that the locals built up manually in order to achieve the 1,000 foot height needed for mountain status and the basis of the Hugh Grant movie *The Man Who Went Up a Hill and Came Down a Mountain*? Sadly no, but finding out the true story (the tumulus on top dates back a lot earlier than Hugh) was fun. I found out about the first animal welfare sanctuary in Britain, and how the so-called peace walls of Belfast look from the top of the Black Mountain. The answer being that they seem petty and trivial when compared to the grandeur of Loch Neagh or the vast curve of Belfast Bay.

But that, though, leads me on to the things I did learn as I walked the skylines of various cities with these different groups of people. I learned that whilst walking alone can be a particular pleasure and tell us much about ourselves, walking with others can tell us much about people. And one lesson I learned is that we are more alike than we are different, something which becomes apparent when we leave our desks and kitchens and get out into freer, more natural surrounds.

The people I met were a gloriously mixed bag: a political researcher who gave me some great insider gossip from Westminster; a Christian copper; a woman who had turned to walking to help heal the wounds from the loss of a child; a young Asian man with special needs; an elderly Brummie lady who, for some reason, called me Jimmy; a retired female teacher from the Black Country. It was this last fellow walker who said something genuinely inspiring to me as we dropped down from Beacon Hill in the Lickeys with its panoramic vistas of the Birmingham suburbs.

She indicated the straggling, chatty hotchpotch that made up our group that day – retirees like her from the outskirts of the city, others members of a community group from the inner city district of Balsall Heath – and said, 'People think of walkers and it's always people like me I suppose, genteel middle-class folks with time on their hands in nice anoraks. But it's for everyone. Birmingham is one of the most rich and diverse cities in the world. And when I go walking I want to be with a group that reflects that. We're all different but we all have one thing in common; we're Brummies who love our city and the countryside around it.'

Some people will dismiss such a sentiment as 'politically correct', a fashionable thing to do amongst the kind of person who would rather sneer and whinge than enthuse or extol. However I thought it was a terrifically heart-gladdening thing to hear and one that we as walkers and lovers of the country should embrace. The British countryside is not the preserve of any one group. It doesn't belong to anyone simply by dint of being born in the region, nor for having the right gear or education or accent or ethnicity. When we think of 'an outdoors type', some will always have a mental image of Barbour jackets and stout boots, walking sticks and bounding Labradors. But in reality, as far as I can see, Gore-Tex is a great leveller, as are jeans and T-shirts and whatever other gear gets pressed into service by walkers as they head for the hills and towpaths, country parks and forests.

Forests are especially pertinent and timely here. When the Government mooted the notion of selling off our woodlands into private hands, what stunned them into an abrupt retreat was not just the volume of the voices raised in protest but the range, everyone from retired colonels to *Socialist Worker* sellers. Just as the views of our cities from the high hills have shown me, we are different, yes, but under our tweeds and breathable layers, our fleeces and football tops, we are also very alike.

Index

STUART MACONIE

Stuart Maconie is a writer and broadcaster known to millions through his best-selling books and radio and TV work. A former deputy editor of the *New Musical Express* (*NME*), he has presented shows on most BBC radio networks and currently presents the afternoon show on 6Music. His *Freak Zone* show, exploring the furthest and wildest shores of pop, is a global cult from St Petesburg to Tel Aviv. He writes regularly for publications as diverse as *Country Walking*, the *Daily Mirror*, the *Radio Times* and the *New Statesman*. His books have sold almost a million copies, and have been translated into Italian, Russian, German and Japanese.

NICK HALLISSEY

Nick Hallissey was dragged across the South Downs Way by his parents at the age of four, and liked it enough to join *Country Walking* magazine 30 or so years later. Along the way he has explored the length and breadth of Britain's footpaths from the Cornish coast to the Cairngorms. He and his colleagues invite fellow adventurous souls to do the same every month in Britain's best-loved walking magazine.

A DAVID & CHARLES BOOK
© F&W Media International, Ltd 2012

David & Charles is an imprint of F&W Media
International, Ltd
Brunel House, Forde Close, Newton Abbot, TQ12 4PU, UK

F&W Media International, Ltd is a subsidiary of
F+W Media, Inc.,
10151 Carver Road, Cincinnati OH45242, USA

Source material courtesy of *Country Walking* magazine
© Bauer Consumer Media 2012

First published in the UK and US in 2012
Digital edition published in 2012

Layout of digital editions may vary depending on reader
hardware and display settings.

A catalogue record for this book is available from the
British Library.

ISBN-13: 978-1-4463-0165-4 Paperback
ISBN-10: 1-4463-0165-6 Paperback

ISBN-13: 978-1-4463-5573-2 e-pub
ISBN-10: 1-4463-5573-X e-pub

ISBN-13: 978-1-4463-5572-5 PDF
ISBN-10: 1-4463-5572-1 PDF

10 9 8 7 6 5 4 3 2 1

Senior Editor: Verity Muir
Senior Designer: Jodie Lystor
Proofreader: Freya Dangerfield
Production Manager: Beverley Richardson

Paperback edition printed in Finland by Bookwell for:
F&W Media International, Ltd
Brunel House, Forde Close, Newton Abbot, TQ12 4PU, UK

F+W Media publishes high quality books on a wide range
of subjects.
For more great book ideas visit: www.fwmedia.co.uk